# Praise for *Digital Detangler*

"A super-engaging book: intimate, personal, at times funny and others sad. But all the time full of practical ideas and activities to help you detangle."

RAFAEL A. CALVO, PhD
Author of *Positive Computing*

"*Digital Detangler* offers practical advice and functional ways to be technologically mindful. Each section acts as a guide to help create more meaningful interactions with our devices, by reclaiming our time and developing obtainable goals for digital wellness."

KATHERINE DROTOS CUTHBERT
Student Wellbeing Coordinator, Vanderbilt University

"Directing your attention to *Digital Detangler* may be the best investment you could make for your time and wellbeing into perpetuity. Amidst a growing chorus of tech and self-help gurus, *Digital Detangler* stands out as a practical immersion into a better way of relating with technology."

ANDREW DUNN
CEO and Co-Founder of Siempo

"So many of us hate how much we stare at our screens but feel powerless to change it. The truth is, technology today is intentionally designed to be addictive; breaking the habit requires thoughtful scrutiny, intelligent analysis, and a hands-on approach. This practical, inspirational book offers a proven method that combines gentle awareness with real-life lesson plans. If information is power, this book is your roadmap to freedom from the endless scroll. *Digital Detangler* offers the why, the how, and the what-to-do-about-it-now. Want to engage more with your real life? Put down your phone, and pick up this book."

LIZA KINDRED
Founder of Mindful Technology

"In *Digital Detangler*, Pete Dunlap has provided a treasure trove of concrete and practical steps that you can begin using immediately to be more focused, productive, and in control of how you use technology. And he backs it up with the latest science, a sense of humor, and a whole lot of heart. The questionnaires and worksheets make it feel like Pete is by your side as your personal guide to making your technology work for you—instead of the other way around."

ROBERT PLOTKIN
Founder of Technology for Mindfulness

"Software and hardware are great tools, but we all need to spend more time figuring out how to preserve our humanware, our precious brain that we pelt with pixels all day and all night long. This book will help you by providing clear, easy-to-use strategies to stay productive and healthy in a tech-rich world."

LARRY D. ROSEN, PhD
Professor Emeritus and Author of *The Distracted Mind*

"The gift of reconnecting our lives through a more physical and palpable existence leaves me hopeful. Bringing his real life into the text will show folks the reality of what is going on in our society. The tools provided will help people of all ages. It is well thought out and a perfect teaching tool. A very readable/workable book."

CARMEN TOUSSAINT
Executive Director of Rivendell Writers' Colony

# DEDICATION

*to all the kids growing up without Cora*
*they'll need all the help they can get*

# CONTENTS

PROLOGUE ix

INTRODUCTION xv

1  BEGIN: Installing Personal Tracking Software  1

2  STRATEGIZE: Goal Setting for the Online Addict  13

3  CONNECT: Social Media Matters  33

4  FOCUS: The Art of Monotasking  63

5  CLARIFY: Pairing Tools with Tasks  91

6  RECLAIM: Purposeful Leisure  107

7  PROTECT: Reducing Your Digital Footprint  127

8  RESTYLE: An Internet as Unique as You  153

9  BE: Creating Space for Non-Doing  183

ACKNOWLEDGEMENTS  195

# PROLOGUE

*We've become a culture of technicians. We're all into the "how" of it and nobody's stepping back and saying, "But why?"*

JOEL SALATIN

First off, none of my work in digital wellness was my original plan. I majored in physics in college at least in part because when you say you majored in physics in college, people say, "Oh wow... physics." The only problem was that I didn't want a job in physics. I'd had some incredible experiences traveling and wanted to find a route out of my hometown.

So, I got a master's degree in education and found a job teaching science in the one place I knew my wife wouldn't refuse: London. After that year, we spent a year in St. Croix in the U.S. Virgin Islands and then a year in Quito, Ecuador. Despite the many incredible experiences along the way, deep down I never believed I could make a career in secondary education. For starters, the emotional labor of teaching is staggering. The ratio of importance to society versus prestige of role is all sorts of janky.

I also began to notice some things that bothered me. I was teaching "digital natives" and assumed they were good with technology. I was wrong. My students couldn't reinstall drivers for the printer, write macros for their spreadsheets, or close an application without using the mouse. I realized that something curious had happened. As a society, we had mistakenly assumed that more time spent with technology meant more technical skills. One of my principals repeatedly pushed us to redefine the role of teacher because—as he pointed to his smartphone—with the knowledge of the world in everyone's pocket, what purpose do teachers still serve? I felt beaten over the head with this idea, but I also became unconvinced of the so-called knowledge my students would find online. Not only is there scant evidence that introducing technology improves comprehension[1], my own experiences bolstered the idea that students were using so-easy-a-monkey-could-use-it platforms mainly to socialize online, not to look up information about physics.

By the time my wife and I settled in Nashville, I was ready to explore a more technical career. I enrolled in a software bootcamp, Nashville Software School.

The software world is about as different from teaching as you can get. If teachers were social and warm and working late, software developers were the opposite. The guy sitting at the desk next to me didn't introduce himself until my second day, which was probably only precipitated by accidental eye contact. The other big difference was the way my coworkers thought about technology. As a teacher, many of my coworkers were unconvinced of technology's learning benefits and were unsure how it fit into their existing lesson plans. Also, most of the teachers I knew had faced technology failures before. For me, it was a projector bulb burning out just as class got underway. The students began to poke each other within about 30 seconds. I

---

[1] Gazzaley and Rosen, *The Distracted Mind.*

realized if I weren't quick on my feet, things were going to feel like *Lord of the Flies* very fast. On the complete opposite end of the spectrum was the pro-tech culture at my software firm. In most of our conversations about users, the prevailing assumption was best articulated by a mentor of mine who called users "an unfortunate requirement of software." Despite the jarring cultural mores, the job paid well and was less stressful than teaching, and I didn't have to plan trips to the bathroom around other people.

Another facet of the transition between education and software was the day's structure. As a teacher, most of my day was structured, often down to the minute. When I became a software developer, I was handed one of the most expensive laptops money can buy, with a high-speed internet connection to boot, and was given large swaths of time to "do work." I struggled mightily to maintain focus. Coworkers recommended strategies, and I sought out tools that could keep me on task. I read productivity books and started setting daily goals. Where there was no structure, I built structure around myself, not because I'm inherently *good* at staying focused—rather, the opposite: without structure I couldn't get anything done. Something big was about to happen in my personal life, though.

After four years of marriage, my wife and I had started anticipating children. Unfortunately, 18 months later, it was still just the two of us. Admittedly, this hit my wife harder than it hit me. Late one night while she was upset, I made a huge mistake. As ashamed as I am to admit it today, I began a sentence with the phrase, "You know what your problem is…?" Never do that. But I did, and I followed it up by accusing my wife of spending too much time on her laptop. Needless to say, that did not go over well, which left me in a no-man's-land where I still felt correct but didn't know what to do with that feeling. Realizing my blunder, the next morning I set about righting the wrong. Although I'm embarrassed to admit it, I set up a program for my wife called "Pete-stakes." If she kept her personal screen time to under 10 hours per week (one hour per weekday and 2.5 hours per weekend day), I'd buy her a massage each week. There was even a grand prize if she successfully "won" six out of eight weeks. Again, never do this! Creating an incentive system for someone you love is not a good policy. However, within a month, we were pregnant with our first child, our daughter Cora June.

I was convinced that the change in technology usage was responsible for our getting pregnant. I've since found evidence associating technology with stress[2], and stress with time to conception[3]. It felt like a huge "aha" moment for me, so I started reading every book I could find on topics as exotic as the quantified-self movement, social psychology, and human-computer interaction. What I found astonished me. There were people who were all too familiar with the trends I was just becoming aware of. Experts had been warning that screens were disrupting our sleep[4], social media was engineering us for addiction[5], and watching television was still bad for us[6]. At the same time, when I looked around, people seemed to be living in blatant disregard of the current scientific knowledge. I witnessed bars where you couldn't start a conversation because people

---

[2] Volpi, "Heavy Technology Use Linked to Fatigue, Stress and Depression in Young Adults."
[3] McDermott, "Is Long-Term Stress Affecting Your Fertility?"
[4] "Blue Light Has a Dark Side."
[5] Alter, *Irresistible.*
[6] Rosen, "Watching TV Leads to Obesity."

were all on their smartphones. I read statistics about smartphone use as it rose and was amazed it didn't take that time away from time on laptops or time watching television[7]. Instead the time was taken from our sleep and our personal interactions. Something that had started on the margins, on the train or while in line, had taken over a big, ugly chunk of our lives and, for the most part, without much resistance.

Then, our daughter died. We drove to the hospital a few days after our due date when my wife was in labor, chatting excitedly about how there would be three of us on our next car ride. The following week is mostly a blur of horrible. One of my most vivid memories is waking after a few fitful hours of sleep on a half-transitioned hospital couch bed, remembering where I was, and sobbing. I'm not an emotional or fragile person, but this broke me. Having been through such a devastating loss at what was supposed to have been the peak of joy, my thoughts rested on a single one: nothing matters anymore. Once you've reached that point, you look at the world a little differently. Things that weren't options before or that I'd thought were too risky suddenly became possible. While I was torn in two by the loss of my daughter, no part of me regretted her impact on my life.

So, I began planning a new type of business. Although there are people complaining about the dark sides of the internet—as they should be—there aren't a lot of courses or manuals to help people reclaim their time. By taking on the challenges associated with using technology skillfully, I don't just want you to have an interesting tidbit to talk about with friends; I want to give you the tools for recovering from your technology compulsions and addictions. In short, I want to give you your life back.

---

[7] Carr, *Utopia Is Creepy.*

The result is this book, a holistic curriculum that examines the many aspects of your relationship to technology and creates a space for the mindful use of your digital tools. Next, we'll take a quick overview of where we're headed.

# INTRODUCTION

*Man is the only kind of varmint [that] sets his own trap, baits it, and then steps in it.*

JOHN STEINBECK

The wind howled as Jack and I approached Eagle Pass for the second time. A couple of days prior, we'd left optimistically from a Canadian state park. We knew there would be snow, but it was July—and to a couple of brothers from the South, how much snow could there really be anyway? The answer: a lot. We'd spent the better part of two days slogging through knee-deep snow drifts, and the day before had culminated in a heated exchange while on the side of an extremely steep ridge. Jack suggested we needed to take a break and think through our plans. The afternoon snow had grown soft, so each step meant sinking to our shins, and losing our footing would mean a hundred-foot fall. I was frustrated with our slow progress and suggested we climb straight up the snowy ridge and over exposed rocks. Jack disagreed. At this point I looked at him and said, "I've got to see what's up there." He looked straight back at me and said, "That's the kind of shit people say before they die." I went up anyway. I stopped before dying, though, and rested on a rock, thought existential thoughts, and then decided we needed to go home. That wouldn't be easy, though. We'd gotten ourselves pretty deep in the hard-to-reach Cascade Mountains of Washington state. We took refuge downhill where we could get water and camp for the night. The next day, all we cared about was getting out of there alive, which was starting to look more challenging than expected. Winds had picked up and as we climbed toward Eagle Pass, it began to rain, sleet, and then snow. On a brief break, Jack looked at me and said, "I'm cold." I replied, "I know, me too." Then, through chattering teeth, he said, "I'm really cold, man. How do you tell if it is an emergency?" I looked at him and shouted above the weather, "This is ALL an emergency!" So began another day and a half of scrambling through a slippery forest of rocks and snow. We eventually made it out, but that moment when Jack asked if it was an emergency stuck with me. How could I have been so oblivious to the dangers we were facing only the day before, and yet so sure we were in an actual emergency the very next day?

Meanwhile, as a society we are reaching a similar crisis point. Americans are now spending 60 hours on screens per week[8]; we are on screens for longer than we are asleep[9]. Smartphones are only about 10 years old, and we are now spending more than 43 days a year (24-hour days) on them[10]. That means millions of us are giving up a month and a half of our year to our smartphones. Television time continues to rise as well. As of 2009, we were spending 76 days per year watching television[11]. To make matters worse, stress levels are rising; self-reported stress levels

---

[8] "The U.S. Digital Consumer Report."
[9] Davies, "We Now Spend More Time on Phones and Laptops than We Do SLEEPING."
[10] "How Much Time Do People Spend on Their Mobile Phones in 2017?"
[11] Rosen, "Watching TV Leads to Obesity."

are up 10-30% in the past three decades[12]. Social isolation continues to tick up as well; today 40% of Americans experience chronic loneliness[13]. Smartphones have been implicated in a number of ways. Studies have correlated and more recently demonstrated a causal relationship between social media use and depression[14]. Even the presence of a smartphone nearby has been shown to be detrimental to interpersonal relationships[15] and our thinking ability[16]. Economically, we've witnessed a massive changing of the guard; today all five of the world's largest companies are tech firms[17]. To give a concrete example, Amazon is so dominant in online retail, it does more than five times the volume of its closest competitor, Walmart[18]. Think about that. Walmart is the little guy. If you didn't know any better, you'd think this is some apocalyptic movie plot where no one can figure out what is happening as our civilization descends into chaos. At this point, I feel safe in saying, this is ALL an emergency!

Hopefully you are on board with the general direction I'm heading here, even if you have some reservations about my telling you not to watch season 7 of *Scandal.*

## ASSUMPTIONS I'M MAKING ABOUT YOU

In full disclosure, I'm making a few assumptions about you:

### You don't want to be judged.

---

[12] Neal, "Stress Levels Soar in America by up to 30% in 30 Years."
[13] Ilardi, "Why Personal Tech Is Depressing."
[14] Twenge, *IGen.*
[15] Lin, "How Your Cell Phone Hurts Your Relationships."
[16] Ward et al., "Brain Drain."
[17] Meeker, "2017 Internet Trends Report."
[18] Wahba, "Amazon Is the King of Online Retail and It's Not Even Close."

Many of us judge ourselves or feel judged by others based on the ways we use our smartphones. This judgment won't solve any problems. By judging ourselves or our loved ones, we just build up resentment that has to be let out at some point. Furthermore, look around. If the majority of people in society have the same issue, it isn't a personal failing on your part or your loved one's part. One more thing: being judgy isn't even effective. Studies about procrastination and problematic drinking have found that beating yourself up actually makes you more likely to fail again in the near future[19].

## You care about what you do with your time.

My mom always said that love was spelled t-i-m-e. That is fine when embroidered on a napkin, but that can be scary once we start to look deeply into where our time goes. What if your time is going to a fruit slicing game on your smartphone? Taking inventory of where your time goes will reveal surprises—and opportunities to reclaim fragments of your life that you thought had slipped away.

## You overuse your smartphone and binge watch television.

Smartphones are engineered to keep you hooked, and television has become more gripping as well. It only takes two episodes of *The Walking Dead* to get more than 70% of viewers to watch the remainder of the season[20]. Tech companies and television producers have analytics that pinpoint exactly when and why you might be tempted to turn them off, and they invest massive amounts of money to keep that from happening.

---

[19] Rodriguez, "Negative Emotions Are Key to Well-Being."
[20] Alter, *Irresistible*.

## You want solutions.

It is easy to complain about the state of affairs. There is plenty of science to back up the idea that the world is going into the crapper. Anyone can throw stones, but you want some ideas for how to regain control of your digital wellness. You want practical tools and techniques designed to help you now, not someday.

## You don't care about what I care about.

Digital wellness has become my all-consuming passion, but you probably don't care about it as much as I do. I don't blame you. You want to take a bit of time to address this issue and then go back to living the virtuous, awesome life you were living before distractions crowded out your best intentions. You will have to dedicate some effort, especially early on, but after several weeks, you'll have solidified your brand-new, good habits. Then, you should be able to turn your attention back toward finding a mate, writing greeting cards, learning to slalom ski, or whatever else you'd rather be doing.

## You know that technology is not just a tool.

You may have heard people say that technology is simply a tool that can be used for good or for ill. If you look at technology on a macro scale, this makes sense. After all, we can use nuclear advances to generate power or build bombs. This idea argues that we hold a tool's user responsible for the way the tool is used, not the tool itself. If you start discussing gun politics with everyone you encounter—something I don't recommend—you'll inevitably meet someone who says, "Guns don't kill people; people kill people." In one sense, that argument is correct. It is a bit more complicated than that, though. Tools aren't just tools; they make certain behaviors easier to carry out. Since they make certain behaviors easier, they are inevitably biased toward certain outcomes. Sure, you can unlock a door with a gun (I've seen plenty of movies where they did just that), but keys are a better tool for the job. When using individual technologies, it is important to make careful observations of what behaviors they bias us toward and to decide whether we like the results. When we are upset with the results, we have every right to either stop using a technology or to demand it be rebuilt with our considerations in mind. That stance doesn't make you anti-technology; rather, it makes you an engaged and informed user of technology.

## TATTOOS & NAIL TRIMMING

I firmly believe there are two types of truth: tattoos and nail trimming. The first, tattoos, represent truth you only need to experience once. When you found out how your coffee machine worked, you didn't leave the manual on the table for easy reference. Like a tattoo, you only need to go through it once, and it lasts forever. Examples of this truth tend to be technical in nature (e.g., a fact that only needs to be memorized once, or a process that is essentially mastered upon one completion). The other type of truth is the nail trimming kind. No matter how many times you cut your nails, they grow back and you have to trim them again. You take the trash out, it fills up, and out it must go again. This type of truth must be tended to regularly if it is to hold any sway in your life. Examples of this truth tend to be transient in nature. Think of kindness, heroism, and most skills. These are the hard ones because you never really finish.

Most of the skills and techniques discussed in the following chapters fall into the nail trimming category of truth. They are only alive as long as you continue putting them into practice. If some of the things I ask you to do are a bit demanding, that is for good reason. Living a good life is demanding. Life isn't all hard, and there is often cause for celebration—but it isn't just sunshine and panda videos. All that said, I have a feeling you are up to the task.

## DESIGNING FOR SUCCESS

This book is broken into nine distinct sections. I've taken this approach because I know firsthand how frustrating it can be to try and implement too many improvements at once. When I was growing up, at Thanksgiving our extended family would go on a biennial golfing trip. So far, so good, right? Until I, the youngest golfer, stepped up to the tee, and my grandfather, grandmother, uncle, dad, and brother would each give me a small piece of advice. "Keep your shoulders flat." "Swing through the ball." "Six iron might be better from this distance." Trying to put all of those pieces of advice into practice, even though they were mostly good advice, became overwhelming and eventually I tuned out. I decided I didn't care how I golfed. Needless to say, when I later tried out for the high school golf team, I didn't make it past the first day. In order to help you escape a similar fate in the digital world, we'll take our time, focusing our efforts on just one aspect of your digital wellness before moving to the next. Here's what our journey will look like:

### Begin: Installing Personal Tracking Software

This section focuses on why our current technology usage needs improving. You'll master the technologies that we'll use to analyze current habits and to make informed decisions moving forward.

### Strategize: Goal Setting for the Online Addict

Nothing risked, nothing gained. You'll place a bet on yourself and will hold yourself accountable to achieving your goals.

### Connect: Social Media Matters

Learn about the economics of social media and the unwritten rules that are redefining our social landscape. Evaluate your behavior, and alter your role in your social environment to maximize your impact without wasting time.

### Focus: The Art of Monotasking

Explore psychology's latest advances in attention and cognitive control. Find ways to group similar tasks and identify your "avocado" tasks.

### Clarify: Pairing Tools with Tasks

This session is packed with tips and tricks for becoming a power user of your devices. Whether on your mobile device or laptop, you'll have clear responsibilities for each device and will optimize your productivity.

### Reclaim: Purposeful Leisure

Whether you rock climb or play bridge, we'll look for ways to increase your enjoyment and investment of time in your hobbies. If you're too busy for hobbies, we'll work to identify your professional goals and will make space to achieve them without burning out.

### Protect: Reducing Your Digital Footprint

Corporations and Uncle Sam have a keen interest in your digital moves. Protect yourself from the worst types of surveillance, and opt out when possible.

## Restyle: An Internet as Unique as You

Email, websites, and apps push into our lives with a lot of baggage. You will change the game by diverting the flow of email and by deconstructing parts of websites that don't appeal.

## Be: Creating Space for Non-Doing

Being alone can be difficult. It is no exaggeration to say that some of us fear solitude. You'll get a taste of gratitude and mindfulness as tools for reducing stress and strengthening your awareness and enjoyment of the present.

## HOW TO USE THIS BOOK EFFECTIVELY

Like many endeavors, the more effort you put into this digital wellness journey, the more you'll get out of it. So, this book will be most effective when you complete the activities, install the diagnostic tools, and answer the prompts provided.

I highly recommend working through the book in a group or with an accountability partner. Plain and simple, it's easier to fall off the wagon when no one's holding you to your goals. Plus, the camaraderie of a friend or book club is a benefit in itself.

I suggest reading one chapter per week. Since you'll set goals at the end of each chapter, I want you to have enough time to take a stab at those goals before proceeding to the next chapter. Even better, you might realize one of your goals was not only achievable but is becoming a habit!

All that said, I recognize that readers have different paces, preferences, or lifestyle constraints. Do what you can, and please don't beat yourself up (or give up) if you do not follow this book perfectly. If you move the needle toward wellness, your efforts are worth it.

My hope is that you'll experience positive and lasting changes, whether they're explicit via your accomplished goals, or more subtle and subjective, like feeling calmer or less distracted. So, what are we waiting for? Let's get started!

# ONE

## BEGIN: Installing Personal Tracking Software

*Every man lives in two realms, the internal and the external. The internal is that realm of spiritual ends expressed in art, literature, morals and religion. The external is that complex of devices, techniques, mechanisms and instrumentalities by means of which we live. Our problem today is that we have allowed the internal to become lost in the external. We have allowed the means by which we live to outdistance the ends for which we live. So much of modern life can be summarized in that suggestive phrase of Thoreau: 'Improved means to an unimproved end.' This is the serious predicament, the deep haunting problem, confronting modern man.*

### MARTIN LUTHER KING, JR.

I'd like to tell you that admitting you have a problem is going to be the hardest part, but that would be a lie. It is my belief that the great truths of our lives are often hidden in plain sight. Deep down, we often know where we stand with others and ourselves, long before we ever look hard into the eyes of uncertainty and make a change. You will face grand ambivalence as you move forward in your attempt to manage your digital life. After all, most of the people around you will keep on scrolling and scrolling, right next to you. Think of yourself as someone who is planning to get sober, but over the past 10 years every public space turned into a bar. You can't easily go cold turkey on the digital world anymore. There are places and activities you must avoid to build a healthy digital life, but you'll still have to order your drink at the bar where all of the booze is sold. It's no easy feat to walk into the bar where all of your old friends are still hanging out, and order a Shirley Temple.

Supposing that last paragraph didn't scare you off, you're going to need to take stock of how ready you are to make a change in your digital experiences. I've provided some space below for you to write down the pros and cons of your current behavior online. You don't have to show this to anyone, so be completely honest with yourself. The cons might be easier to list out since they annoy us, but the pros are there. After all, if there were only cons to your current choices, you'd be a pretty irrational person.

### Continuing My Current Online Behavior

| PROS | CONS |
| --- | --- |
|  |  |
|  |  |
|  |  |
|  |  |

Now, look through the list of pros. Circle any of the pros that are exclusive to the digital realm. These are the things that are important to you and that you'll probably need to keep doing online. The non-circled pros can be experienced elsewhere. For example, if you've listed seeing pictures of your family, that would probably need to be circled. On the other hand, if one of your pros is interacting with friends, you shouldn't circle that. There are lots of ways to spend time with friends that aren't mediated by technology. Hopefully this exercise shows you that many of the benefits of time online aren't exclusively available through a smartphone or laptop.

It's time to figure out just how strong your addiction to your smartphone really is. You'll use something called a nomophobia (fear of being without your smartphone) questionnaire to place yourself on a scale that ranges from 20 to 140. Before you respond to the survey, go ahead and take a guess about where you'll fall.

**Nomophobia Score Prediction:**

## Nomophobia Questionnaire[21]

| Respond to the following statements on a scale of 1 (strongly disagree) to 7 (strongly agree). | 1 | 2 | 3 | 4 | 5 | 6 | 7 |
|---|---|---|---|---|---|---|---|
| I would feel uncomfortable without constant access to information through my smartphone. | O | O | O | O | O | O | O |
| I would be annoyed if I could not look up information on my smartphone when I wanted to do so. | O | O | O | O | O | O | O |
| Being unable to get the news (e.g., happenings, weather) on my smartphone would make me nervous. | O | O | O | O | O | O | O |
| I would be annoyed if I could not use my smartphone and/or its capabilities when I wanted to do so. | O | O | O | O | O | O | O |
| Running out of battery in my smartphone would scare me. | O | O | O | O | O | O | O |

[21] "Are You a Nomophobe?"

4

| | | | | | | | |
|---|---|---|---|---|---|---|---|
| If I were to run out of credits or hit my monthly data limit, I would panic. | O | O | O | O | O | O | O |
| If I did not have a data signal or could not connect to Wi-Fi, then I would constantly check to see if I had a signal or could find a Wi-Fi network. | O | O | O | O | O | O | O |
| If I could not use my smartphone, I would be afraid of getting stranded somewhere. | O | O | O | O | O | O | O |
| If I could not check my smartphone for a while, I would feel a desire to check it. | O | O | O | O | O | O | O |

**If I did not have my smartphone with me,**

| | | | | | | | |
|---|---|---|---|---|---|---|---|
| I would feel anxious because I could not instantly communicate with my family and/or friends. | O | O | O | O | O | O | O |
| I would be worried because my family and/or friends could not reach me. | O | O | O | O | O | O | O |
| I would feel nervous because I would not be able to receive text | O | O | O | O | O | O | O |

| | | | | | | | |
|---|---|---|---|---|---|---|---|
| messages and calls. | | | | | | | |
| I would be anxious because I could not keep in touch with my family and/or friends. | ○ | ○ | ○ | ○ | ○ | ○ | ○ |
| I would be nervous because I could not know if someone had tried to get a hold of me. | ○ | ○ | ○ | ○ | ○ | ○ | ○ |
| I would feel anxious because my constant connection to my family and friends would be broken. | ○ | ○ | ○ | ○ | ○ | ○ | ○ |
| I would be nervous because I would be disconnected from my online identity. | ○ | ○ | ○ | ○ | ○ | ○ | ○ |
| I would be uncomfortable because I could not stay up to date with social media and online networks. | ○ | ○ | ○ | ○ | ○ | ○ | ○ |
| I would feel awkward because I could not check my notifications for updates from my connections and online networks. | ○ | ○ | ○ | ○ | ○ | ○ | ○ |
| I would feel anxious because I could not check | ○ | ○ | ○ | ○ | ○ | ○ | ○ |

| | | | | | | | |
|---|---|---|---|---|---|---|---|
| my email messages. | | | | | | | |
| I would feel weird because I would not know what to do. | ○ | ○ | ○ | ○ | ○ | ○ | ○ |
| Total Score: | | | | | | | |

Once you've filled in all the bubbles, go ahead and total up your score; each answer has a point value representing your agreement (e.g., an answer of 6 is worth six points toward your total). Now look at where you are on the range from 20 to 140. This isn't *Cosmopolitan*, so I'm not giving you five different paragraphs to tell you how to feel based on your responses. I want you to decide for yourself. Do your results surprise you? How close was your prediction to your results?

## MEASURE THYSELF

How well do you know your habits? Could you reliably estimate how much time you spend online? Or what time of day you are most likely to watch Netflix? Or how your weekend smartphone use compares to your weekday use? Without making a detailed inventory of your time online, it doesn't make much sense to start making big changes to the way you use your devices. Until you know exactly where your intentions melt into indulgence, you'll have a hard time changing in meaningful or sustainable ways.

If you are like most people, you know a little bit about your habits but probably have never done a thorough accounting of where your time really goes online. You may already have a good sense of where your time goes, but be prepared to be surprised at how the time adds up. One client of mine was on track to spend 25 days (day and night) of the next year on just the Facebook app on her smartphone. My brother found out he was going to spend more than 45 days of 2018 on his smartphone if he didn't make any changes. Think of all the things you wish you could do but just "never have the time" to do.

The great news is that peering behind the digital curtain is now easier than ever. An application called RescueTime (rescuetime.com) installs on nearly any device (Windows, OSX, Linux, and Android) and quietly records what you are doing at all times. If that sounds creepy, it should. Fortunately, the company has a stellar reputation for not exploiting your data and allows you to permanently delete your data at the click of a button. I've spoken to the engineer who created the deletion script, and it really does delete all of your data. Once you've installed it, RescueTime will begin watching your movements and will automatically calculate a productivity score for you. This number is useful to glance at throughout your week. It provides feedback to any adjustments you make. For example, does starting work earlier mean you are more or less productive? Do your distractions pull you away from meaningful work for long periods or in short spurts? Those types of questions become answerable once you have data to back up your conclusions.

*Figure 1 RescueTime provides rich reports detailing your digital activities.*

RescueTime automatically categorizes most sites and apps along a productivity scale from very unproductive to very productive. For the most part, those categorizations are pretty spot-on. Twitter isn't really productive, after all. Take a few moments, though, and adjust the categories to your own individual circumstances. Maybe you are a video editor and often publish to YouTube as part of your day job. By default, RescueTime would consider all time on YouTube as unproductive. To avoid this problem, spend 10-15 minutes on the RescueTime site (rescuetime.com/categories) tweaking your categories' productivity ratings to make sure they line up with your conceptions of productivity.

There is one final step to get your RescueTime setup to provide you with the best feedback possible. After installing RescueTime on all of your devices, let data accumulate for about a week. Then visit a special page on the site that displays only your activities that RescueTime was unable to automatically categorize (rescuetime.com/categorize/activities?show_only_uncategoriz ed=true). Starting at the top, categorize your uncategorized activities by either selecting the category they best fit in or by directly rating their productivity. Don't worry about categorizing every single uncategorized activity; just make sure any site or app that you visit regularly is categorized. Once you've finished categorizing, your RescueTime data will be as accurate as possible. You are ready to start taking a deeper look at your data.

If you are an Apple user, you may have noticed that RescueTime does not support iOS devices. Unfortunately, Apple has decided that for the foreseeable future it will not allow any app to view usage data of other apps. On the bright side, there is still a way to collect app usage information on an iOS device. An app called Moment (inthemoment.io) reminds you to take screenshots of your app usage (only available in the battery section of the settings) periodically and updates visualizations of your smartphone use. It also collects other interesting information like how often you pick up and look at your smartphone each day and the total amount of time you spend on your smartphone each day.

*Figure 2  Moment makes it easy to see how you are using your iOS device.*

While RescueTime and Moment can handle most devices, what about measuring gaming or television watching? Unfortunately, there is no easy way to measure usage of gaming consoles or television. The best approach currently available is to power your console or television through a smart plug, which monitors and reports how long electronics powered through the plug were used.

## IF I ONLY HAD MORE TIME...

Before we go any further, take a moment to remember why you'd like to use your technology more mindfully in the first place. What would you do if you had more time? Are there items on your to-do list that never get done? Do you have any abandoned hobbies you'd like to reinstate? Dreams to pursue? Connections to make?

**If I had more time, I would like to:**

**1.**



**2.**



**3.**



In the next chapter, you'll identify your habits and leverage something called the Fundamental Attribution Error to make bad habits easier to replace.

# TWO

## STRATEGIZE: Goal Setting for the Online Addict

*I bought a safe with a timed combination lock. It is basically the most useful artifact in my life. I leave my phone and my router cable in my safe so I'm completely free of any interruption and I can spend the entire day, weekend or week reading and writing... To circumvent my safe I have to open a panel with a screwdriver, so I have to hide all my screwdrivers in the safe as well. So, I would have to leave home to buy a screwdriver—the time and cost of doing this is what stops me.*

EVGENY MOROZOV

By now you've installed RescueTime or Moment. You are eager to look at your results, but I encourage you to hold off for a few days. If you look at your results too quickly, you are prone to see data that is highly skewed by a small sample size. In order to accurately understand your technology habits, allow at least a week or two of data to accumulate. For now, we'll take a brief look at how habits operate in our daily lives. Then, we'll examine methods of behavior change that fail, and we'll diagnose where they go wrong. Finally, I'll unveil a key to lasting behavior change.

## HABITS

Habits can be fickle things. Why do we do what we do? How come some of us—not me—floss every single day, while others of us don't seem to have the willpower to get off the sofa (after all, this latest season of *Game of Thrones* isn't going to watch itself)? The key to habits is momentum. As we all learned in physics class, an object in motion tends to stay in motion, and an object at rest tends to stay at rest. Our habits operate in much the same way. Good and bad habits tend to persist through their own inertia.

If that all sounds pretty theoretical, let me offer a concrete example. A week after graduating high school, my best friend and I flew to Maine and began hiking the Appalachian Trail toward Georgia. We hiked in just about every type of weather and slept everywhere from tents to dirt floors to picnic tables. When we finished the trip, friends and family wanted to hear about our adventure, how we'd managed to keep hiking day after day. To them, we were Herculean in our ability to travel for so long, with everything we needed on our backs. The truth of the matter is, the first month *was* rough. My friend hurt his knee early on, and we were more than a little terrified of what we'd signed on for. Our packs were heavy and we were terribly sore. Waking up to rain on your tent with legs still sore from the day before, no real option other than to hike—you only have enough food to get you to the next town—took its toll on us. Both of us cried at some point during the first month. Then something happened. Habit took over. Our legs strengthened, and we mailed home unnecessary items. We adapted to the environment we found ourselves in, and the final four and a half months were more fun than our high school lives had been.

The key to changing our habits is to get moving in the right direction. If we are going to change bad habits, we're going to have to apply some force, initially. Before we talk about how to change habits, though, let's look in more depth at how habits function.

## HOW HABITS FUNCTION

All habits have three main components: a trigger, a routine, and a reward[22]. When you experience a trigger, you complete some routine behavior, which then bestows some reward upon you. Because you have been rewarded, you are now more likely to repeat this habit the next time you encounter that same trigger. This pattern is called a habit loop.

See if you can identify the trigger, routine, and reward in each of these examples:

*Your violin sounds bad (trigger), so you tune it (routine), and then it sounds good (reward).*

*You get hungry, so you eat food and feel sated.*

*It is Saturday night, so you go dancing and feel social validation.*

*You go home for the holidays, take part in a family tradition and feel a part of something larger than yourself.*

Once habits are well established, they become automatic and it becomes more difficult to identify the trigger. Furthermore, sometimes rewards don't pan out. In many cases, being unsure you are going to be rewarded following a routine can make you more likely to experience the trigger and routine. A common

---

[22] Duhigg, *The Power of Habit.*

example is gambling behavior; you may pull on the slot machine many times to no effect before you ever win. Similarly, some habits don't seem to have a reward at all. Generally, though, there is something we are hoping for and might achieve. For example, why do we hurt those we love? In the case of arguing with loved ones, perhaps we are hoping to prove ourselves "right" or to take someone else down a few pegs, and that becomes the reward. Maybe we hope the disagreement will reward us with better understanding moving forward. We may not always get the reward, and the reward may not even be admirable, but it is enough to put us through the habit loop again.

## TECHNOLOGY HABITS

In many ways, our online lives mimic our offline ones. Here are a few common habit loops that many of us take part in online:

*A person posts something polemic on social media, so you post an angry rebuttal and feel excited or vindicated when others post to agree with your side.*

*Your phone runs out of battery, so you charge it and regain connection to friends and family.*

*You need to use the toilet, so you play on your phone and feel less bored.*

*You are bored, so you play video games and feel amused.*

Now, we need to reflect on our own technology-mediated behavior. First, come up with a couple of positive technology habit loops. You should identify the trigger that leads you to do something useful with technology, which provides you with some reward.

**Draw your positive technology habit loops here:**

Are there any ways in which you've developed a negative habit loop that is related to your technology use?

**Draw your negative technology habit loops here:**

## WHAT WILL NOT WORK

Armed with this knowledge about habit loops, you might be ready to dive right in and start changing your behavior immediately. As silly as this may sound, take a moment and imagine yourself failing. Think about some habit you want to change. What would it feel like to fail to change it? What are the reasons you may fail to change it?

**Top five reasons I may fail to change my technology habits:**

**1.**

**2.**

**3.**

**4.**

**5.**

Changing our behaviors is one of the hardest things we do, so make sure you think through what you are attempting. Let's consider a few ways changing your behavior can hit a brick wall.

### Silencing Alerts & Notifications

One common piece of advice is to silence alerts and notifications so that you are interrupted less often by your technology. This is great advice, but don't expect this to radically change the way you use technology. We have many habit loops around technology that are much more sophisticated than a simple ding or buzz. In fact, prominent office-environment researcher Dr. Gloria Mark found that three out of four interruptions are internally generated[23]. That means that by silencing alerts and notifications, at best you'll only reduce interruptions by 25%. Although doing so is a noble endeavor, many of us need something a little stronger than a five-minute session with our settings.

## Getting Tech Companies to Change

Another way to change our digital behavior is to have technology companies change the way they design apps and platforms. There is excellent work being done toward this end by a movement Tristan Harris started, Time Well Spent. More recently the movement has evolved into the Center for Humane Technology, which is focused on creating technology industry standards more suited to wellbeing.

By the same token, some might argue that if technology companies are manipulating us (more details on exactly how in Chapter 3), the government must regulate them to protect consumers. I agree with the spirit of both of these arguments, but there are a couple of reasons this book will not focus on these issues. First, the technology companies that have the strongest habit loops are social platforms that are making billions on an advertising-based business model. That may change in the future, but I'm not going to wait around hoping it will. The same goes for the federal gridlock we're experiencing. There are definitely sensible regulations that are needed, but we don't seem very close to a law getting passed.

From a psychological perspective, the best path forward is to maintain an internal locus of control. While you should voice your opinion in public debates and let your elected

---

[23] Gazzaley and Rosen, *The Distracted Mind.*

representatives know where you stand, the best thing you can do for yourself is to take actions within the context of your life. Living with an external locus of control means you are always depending on external circumstances to provide your happiness. When external circumstances disappoint, you become a powerless victim.

## Gritting Your Teeth

This approach seems to be the most common way we attempt habit changes but also one of the most failure-prone. David Rock refers to a study of people with heart conditions in his book *Your Brain at Work*. He relates that only one in nine people faced with a dire need for lifestyle changes was able to make meaningful changes[24]. Most New Year's resolutions fail (92%) because most of us pluck something out of the sky, and that becomes our goal for the new year[25]. We don't stop to make a plan and think through what it will take to make the goal a reality.

. . .

By now, it should be clear that no one is going to fix your bad habits for you and that your first instinct—gritting your teeth—can get you in over your head. With all this doom and gloom, you may be thinking, "How on Earth can I change anything?!?" The next section explains a concept called the Fundamental Attribution Error, which contains a key insight toward meaningful, lasting habit changes.

---

[24] Rock, *Your Brain at Work*.
[25] Diamond, "Just 8% of People Achieve Their New Year's Resolutions. Here's How They Do It."

## FUNDAMENTAL ATTRIBUTION ERROR

The Fundamental Attribution Error is our tendency to overestimate personality factors and to underestimate situational factors in influencing behavior. This concept is most easily explained by looking at a real example.

When my wife and I moved to Nashville, we knew almost no one. Fortunately, we did have a mutual friend, Emily, who graciously offered to introduce us to her friends. One night shortly after arriving in Nashville, she had a party at her condo and invited all of her Nashville friends so that we could make some new connections. If this were a reality show and you had asked her Nashville friends about my wife and me, I believe they would have mentioned that we were shy or timid or withdrawn. But if I were asked to describe my wife and me, I'd never think of shy, timid, or withdrawn. In fact, most of the time I consider myself to be quite outgoing. What is going on here?

In the situation I just described, there are two groups of people: Nashville people and new people (my wife and me). The Nashville people knew everyone at the party except the two new people. On the other hand, my wife and I only knew each other and Emily. If my wife and I seemed shy at the party, it was probably because we were on shaky social footing compared to the rest of Emily's friends, who already knew how to engage with each other without resorting to small talk. The Nashville people knew lots of information about the social landscape, which gave them more options for how to behave.

Think deeply about the Fundamental Attribution Error, and you'll start to see it all around you. Is your toddler screaming in the backseat because he's a fussy kid (personality), or could it be because he's been sitting in his own excrement for a while (situation)? Did your coworker get promoted ahead of you because the manager likes her more (personality), or does she have some experience that makes her more qualified (situation)?

At this point, you're probably coming to appreciate the power of the Fundamental Attribution Error. It can be liberating to realize that when we don't seem to measure up, or we fall short of our goals, there is a situational component that we're probably underestimating. But all of this comes with an unsettling side as well. On a deep level, we depend on the concept of a personality. The Fundamental Attribution Error does not suggest that personalities don't exist; they just don't influence behavior as much as we often expect. While we like to think of ourselves as going from situation A to situation B to situation C and behaving in roughly the same manner, the truth is that much of our behavior depends on the situations in which we find ourselves. Of course, this is obvious at the extremes: you may be an honest person generally, but if you were starving, stealing a loaf of bread becomes a much likelier option. Conversely, even a misogynist could be faithful if stuck on an island with only one partner.

So why do I want you to understand the Fundamental Attribution Error? For this important takeaway: If you want to act a certain way or be a certain type of person, construct an environment around yourself that makes you more likely to act that way or be that type of person. To simplify it even more…

**Be ruthless with your environment,**

**but be compassionate towards yourself.**

Next time you are down on yourself or realize you made the same mistake yet again, look at your failings logically. Let's say you think you are a complete failure. How could we know for sure you are a failure? We'd have to put you in an ideal situation where it is very hard to be a failure and make sure you still failed there. So, stop beating yourself up when you fail. Instead, look at your failures with curiosity. What parts of your environment could be tweaked to help ensure you don't suffer the same result next time? Is there an environment that would allow you to succeed?

This all may be a little hard to sink your teeth into, so I'll give you an example from my days as a software developer. My manager and I were on a walk one day and were talking about habits and exercise. When he revealed that he was a member at two separate gyms, I couldn't believe it. Why on Earth would you pay two monthly gym memberships? He laughed at my disbelief and explained that it isn't often that he feels the I-would-like-to-work-out impulse, so he figured that by joining both, he'd be that much more likely to be close to a gym when he had that feeling. In this way, he was ruthless with his environment—putting multiple gyms around himself—while being compassionate with himself. He knew that everyone has a hard time wanting to work out, and he didn't beat himself up for not having the urge very often.

## HABIT ANALYSIS

At this point, I'm assuming that RescueTime or Moment has been installed for at least a week or so. Your online usage information has been collecting in the cloud, and you are excited to finally find out where your online time is going. I understand your urge to see the data, but making predictions before you check out your stats will make it that much more meaningful when you do look through the data later. Take a moment to answer each of these questions first:

**Which sites or apps do you expect you use most often, and when (e.g., time of day, day of week, time of year)?**

**Which devices do you expect you are using for which types of activities?**

**What pattern do you most expect to see in your data?**

**If a close friend were asked to describe you, what are the three values you most hope he/she would mention?**

1.

2.

3.

Now that you've filled out those questions, we have something to work with. As you look through your data, fill in the questions below and compare your answers to the previous ones.

**Which sites or apps do you use most often, and when (e.g., time of day, day of week, time of year)?**

**Which devices are you using for which types of activities?**

**What surprises you the most?**

**Write the three values that best represent what you spend your online time doing.**

**1.**

**2.**

**3.**

Were you on the mark? Some people have no clue what their online habits are, and others know exactly where their time goes. Being able to accurately guess where your time goes is not the point. The big takeaway here is this: Are you happy with where your time is going?

In this next section, we'll categorize various online activities as things you do either on your smartphone or on your laptop. If you do the activity on both your smartphone and your laptop, put it on both lists and circle it. I'll explain what to do with those circled items in a moment. This is a partial list, so feel free to customize it with your own activities or subcategories (for example, maybe you use Instagram on your smartphone but Twitter on your laptop, or you might use Skype chat on your smartphone but Google Hangouts on your laptop). Add each of these items to the table below:

| | |
|---|---|
| **Online Shopping** | **Banking** |
| **Email** | **Streaming Videos** |
| **Watching TV/Movies** | **Creating a Document** |
| **Surfing the Internet** | **Chat** |
| **Paying Bills** | **Playing Video Games** |
| **Social Media** | **Calendar** |

| SMARTPHONE | LAPTOP |
|---|---|
| | |
| | |
| | |
| | |
| | |
| | |
| | |
| | |
| | |
| | |
| | |
| | |

If you'll indulge me, I'd like to quickly compare smartphones and laptops. The differences may seem obvious, but they have big implications for how we use them. The first major difference is that you nearly always have your smartphone with you. On the other hand, your laptop may often be on, but it's set aside when you are driving or eating. Think of your laptop as a polite friend who can recognize social cues and ducks out of the party before you wish he would leave. Now think of your smartphone as an interesting friend you love to hang out with, but who ultimately wears you out with his stories and makes you late for your next event. Another major difference between a smartphone and a laptop is the keyboard. A smartphone has a tiny, screen-based keyboard. While some people can type quite quickly on them, I've yet to meet someone who can type faster on a smartphone than on a laptop. In fact, because of exactly this issue, Apple released an update to their operating system that allowed users to type text messages from their laptops instead of their phones. At their core, smartphones are media consumption devices. They are great when you are scanning for tiny bits of news stories, or keeping up with the minutiae of your friends' and friends' friends' lives, or even dashing off a quick tweet, or adding a short caption to your selfie—but when you are ready to do real work, most people opt for a laptop. Its expansive keyboard suggests a give-and-take between user and tool. We are encouraged to create on a laptop. As we'll explore further in Chapter 8, your browsing experience is also much more customizable on a laptop.

Hopefully by now you are a committed member of the church of the laptop. If so, I challenge you to take all of the activities in your smartphone list that you circled, and mark through them. You are already taking part in those activities on your laptop, so the only shift will be not doing them on your smartphone any longer. So, go ahead. Delete the app or disconnect your account. It might hurt at first, but don't worry—you aren't doing anything that isn't reversible, should you later change your mind.

## GOALS

Some people hate the word "goal." It brings back memories of boring meetings and bosses who forced you to make pie-in-the-sky goals that you later fell predictably short of, only to find out that your merit increase was squat because you didn't meet your goals. So, if you would like to change the word to something else like "objectives," "intentions," or "aspirations," go ahead.

Seriously, mark through "goals." I won't tell.

We should be smart about this activity, though. If you are going to stick to the goal, there has to be something at stake. A lot of people give themselves rewards for meeting their goals, but I'm going to suggest something a bit outrageous. Instead of giving yourself something if you succeed, think of an organization or person you would hate to donate to if you do not meet your goal. Whether it is your favorite team's rival, an opposing political party, or the roommate who always ate your cereal, pinpoint an entity that disgusts you. Now pick an amount of money that you will donate to this entity if you fail to meet your goals. As ridiculous as this sounds, committing to a behavioral contract like this actually works[26].

Think you've got the hang of goal-setting? Good! This exercise is a recurring feature of this book. At the end of each chapter, I'll ask you to set a goal related to the concepts covered in that chapter. I'd like you to work toward your goal for at least one week before assessing whether or not you achieved it. Then, you'll begin the next chapter, learn new concepts, set a new goal, and the cycle will repeat.

A final word of caution: Don't go crazy on me. If you will need to spend hours (that you don't have) to get these goals accomplished, go back and revise them. If you are used to eating lunch every day with your smartphone and your goal is device-free meals, give yourself two cheat days for the first week. Failing or using up all of your initiative on your first week is not going to help you stay motivated. This isn't a crash diet; it's a whole new lifestyle. We are in it for the long haul. Anyone can go to a cabin without internet for a weekend. We are looking for ways

---

[26] Blanding, "The Business of Behavioral Economics."

to live within the crazy lives we have, not to escape from them.

# SET YOUR GOALS

At this point, we've been talking about how to change your behaviors by redesigning your environment and by making a few changes to your device choices when you go online. Now, it's time to set some concrete goals for the upcoming week.

**If I do not meet my goals, I will give $____ to _____.**

Now that you've decided what is at stake, it's time to choose two goals that will be tied to your wager. Rather than make both of the goals about technology, I recommend picking one goal about technology and another from your own to-do list.

At the end of Chapter 1, you listed things you'd like to do if you had more time; that list is a great place to start for your "to-do list" goal. For instance, finish that tree house, take a walk each day, call your mother, or visit that friend from high school.

If you are having trouble coming up with a technology-related goal, here are a few of my favorite suggestions:

- Keep a paper internet journal (before using your laptop, write down what you are going to do online).

- Spend three consecutive hours doing something screen-less each week.

- Limit personal screen time per day (try one hour on weekdays, 2.5 hours on weekend days).

- Check email no more than twice a day.

- Turn off your device for two hours a day (for some reason this feels different than Do Not Disturb mode).

- Spend five minutes each day learning a new keyboard hot-key (more on hot-keys in Chapter 5).

- Put your Wi-Fi on an outlet timer.

- Remove email/social media from your smartphone.

- Eat meals without devices.

- Call or meet once a week with a close friend.

**My goals are:**

**1.**


**2.**


Up next, we'll explore social media in depth and will observe how it is changing our social landscape. We'll also find ways to use social media without getting carried away.

# THREE

## CONNECT: Social Media Matters

*[Smartphones have] left us with the most distinctive social tic since cigarettes. And cigarettes may be deadly and disgusting, but they're cool and chic too...the sensuous richness of the idea of new information at any moment, and the frothing, blooming world that spins unseen while we fondle our devices in search of something else.*

IAN BOGOST

I hope you were able to meet the goals you set in the last chapter. Either way, keep moving forward. Don't beat yourself up. Try something new when you set a goal at the end of this chapter. Instead of just writing your goal, list three things that need to happen for the goal to be met. That could mean scheduling time to complete the goal in advance, or clearing one of your weekends, or committing to 30 minutes a day of concerted effort. Thinking through what will need to happen from a practical standpoint before committing to your goal will make you much more likely to follow through.

Now, let's turn our attention to social media. We'll start by cataloging some specific techniques social platforms are using to keep us hooked on their products. After that, we'll take a moment to examine the business realities influencing the decisions those platforms make. Then, we'll examine the effects social media has on us, for better and for worse. After looking at social media generally, I'll encourage you to reflect on your own posts and those that make their way into your feeds. This chapter will close with a handful of ways to use social media platforms less, plus advice on how to be more in control when you do log on.

In the last chapter, we took a look at some of our technology habit loops. I want to focus on one in particular, the smartphone loop. In the smartphone loop, you hit a point in your day—sometimes but not always a transition—where you feel bored, listless, or despondent (trigger). Our internal tendency to maximize fun and minimize boredom kicks in and wonders, "Has anyone posted something interesting on social media?" Out comes your phone, where you spend anywhere from a couple of minutes to an hour getting stimulated by the thumb treadmill that is your various social news feeds (routine). The reward for checking your feeds is any amusement or arousal you find in the mixed bag of text, images, and videos.

Eventually, once you've gone through this loop hundreds of times a day[27], it becomes automatic. Your phone becomes another limb, an extension of your mind. You probably don't notice it as long as you don't lose your phone. All of a sudden, the loss reveals a grim dependence driven by thousands of trips through the smartphone loop. Remember my client who was on pace to spend 25 days of her year on her iPhone's Facebook app? Put another way, Facebook alone would take up almost a month of the eight non-sleeping months of her year (assuming

---

[27] Woollaston, "How Often Do YOU Look at Your Phone? The Average User Now Picks up Their Device More than 1,500 Times a Week."

she sleeps for about eight hours per night). In the next section, I'll explore some ways tech companies have designed their products to cement the smartphone loop and keep us from disengaging. Not all of these techniques are inherently evil or manipulative, but they certainly are reasons we come back to our devices again and again.

## SOCIAL MEDIA: THE STRATEGIES

### Novelty

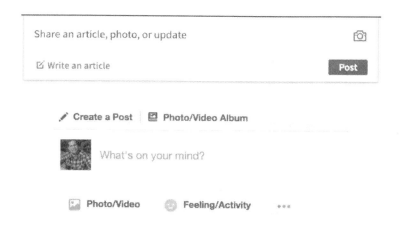

*Figure 3 Social media platforms are always encouraging us to post.*

All of the social platforms (Facebook, Twitter, Instagram, LinkedIn, Pinterest, Snapchat, YouTube, and others) encourage us to share what we are up to. They coax us to post with questions like, "What's on your mind, Pete?" (Facebook) or "What's happening?" (Twitter). By having users generate the content of the news feeds, these platforms guarantee you always have a reason to log on and see what's new—after all, maybe someone you know recently got engaged or bought a fair-trade kitten. Even in this very moment, while you are reading this, you are missing out on all kinds of entertaining posts. The most alluring will not just be text, however. Try posting a text-only post and a photo/video at the same time, and compare your posts' analytics. In terms of your brain's processing speed, photos and videos have a leg up on text. Our brains process imagery up to 60,000 times faster than text[28].

## Streaking

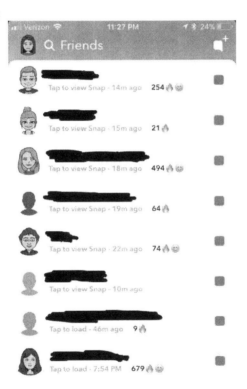

*Figure 4  Snapchat uses flame emojis to indicate streaks in communication.*

---

[28] Galloway, *The Four.*

Streaking is a feature where apps keep track of how many consecutive days you've used the application in a particular way. It could be your meditation app or Snapchat, but chances are you're subtly being encouraged to keep your streak alive. If you and your best friend from college have sent each other messages each day for 679 days straight, are you really going to be the one to throw all that away? I'd read about this but didn't think of it as a big deal until I was recently on a family cruise that went deep enough into the sea that cell signals were nowhere to be found. I knew my cousin used Snapchat, so I asked her if she felt worried about losing her SnapStreaks. She assured me she was not; she'd anticipated this issue and had given a friend her password so her friend could keep up the streaks in her absence. Streaking allows application designers to encourage certain behaviors that happen to be important for their annual reports, namely daily active user (DAU) counts. The days when a company like Nike tried convincing kids that their product was the coolest seem benign now that apps are teaching kids when to communicate.

## Variable Reward

The behaviorists of the 20th century discovered that the best way to condition a particular behavior in lab rats was to provide intermittent rewards[29]. This makes a tremendous amount of sense if you think about things you enjoy. You wouldn't enjoy watching your favorite football team play nearly as much if they were always guaranteed a win. The fact that they could have lost and prevailed despite the other team's best efforts is the special sauce that makes sports so compelling. Variable rewards are used to encourage people to do all kinds of behaviors, from

---

[29] Burkeman, "This Column Will Change Your Life."

pulling the lever on the slots, to flipping open Tinder again, to checking email one final time before bed. Instagram has even been accused of consciously holding back content so that it can give you a "jackpot" of stimulation at opportune moments[30]. In every case, the inherent unpredictability of the reward is what keeps us coming back for more.

## History Augmented Feed

When I mention a history augmented feed, I'm referring to the way platforms use artificial intelligence to gather and organize data about your previous news feed interactions to influence your future content. To break down that idea a bit, consider that many of the social platforms only show you a fraction of the available stories in your news feed. At any given moment on Facebook, users only see around 300 of a potential 1500 current items[31]. How does Facebook decide which 300 posts to put into your feed and which 1200 to hide? For Facebook and others, the answer is artificial intelligence. In this context, artificial intelligence involves using data from past usage (e.g., the types of things you've loved or been outraged by, or clicked like on, or how connected you are to the person who made the post) to make an educated guess at how engaging you will find new content that your friends post. Over time, Facebook gets pretty good at predicting the types of things you'll be into. In fact, one researcher claimed to know a user's personality better than the user's spouse would, based on just 300 "likes"[32]. As far as Facebook is concerned, if it keeps you engaged in the platform,

[30] Price, *How to Break Up with Your Phone.*
[31] Goel, "Facebook Tinkers With Users' Emotions in News Feed Experiment, Stirring Outcry."
[32] Lapowsky, "How Facebook Knows You Better Than Your Friends Do."

it's a win.

## Lock In

*Figure 5 With that many emails, I'm unlikely to change email provider.*

I have not paid for email since my parents bought monthly subscriptions to AOL, back when no one put real names in email addresses—yes, I'm talking about you, fuzzybear1986@aol.com. Gmail swept me off my feet in my college days, and I have since amassed more than 36,000 emails. That means the cost to switch email providers would be huge. What if I switched and a year later I really needed to figure out where I bought that favorite pair of sneakers? I'm out of luck. What if you set up a series of filters to keep junk out of your inbox? You'd have to sink time into recreating the same filters on a new email provider in their new—to you, anyway—interface. We also get accustomed to the look and feel of a particular platform. Try using Bing instead of Google for a few days, and you'll probably notice at least some frustration at minor changes, anything from button placement to color differences.

## Suggested Scrolling & Infinite Scroll

*Figure 6  With so many images cut off, Pinterest is making sure I start scrolling.*

Take a moment and visit a Pinterest page. Notice that the bottom row contains images that are cut off. You'll have to scroll to see the rest of those images. So, you start to scroll, and now you may as well check out a few more rows of images.

*Figure 7 Instagram loading new content into the page in its infinite scroll.*

As you scroll further down, more and more images are automatically loaded for your perusal. You may think this is how the internet has always functioned. However, in the past, content was placed on separate pages, and you had to click the word "Next" to load more. Designers abandoned that strategy once they realized people interacted with the platform for longer when they didn't have a periodic stopping point.

## Endowed Progress Effect

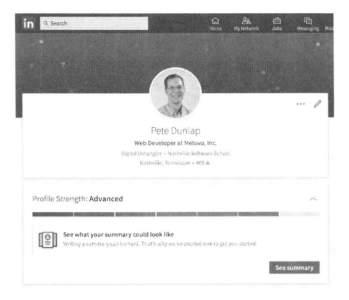

*Figure 8 My profile strength used to say "Weak." After adding more details, LinkedIn now calls my profile "Advanced."*

With a name like that, this one better be good. The Endowed Progress Effect describes our tendency to complete tasks we start and to overvalue our own creations. Many social platforms use this technique to encourage users to fill out their entire profiles. If you've ever signed up for LinkedIn and essentially were told, "We appreciate the effort, but your profile is only mediocre at this time"—you know what I'm talking about. LinkedIn is more than happy to make a few suggestions: add a few more details about your internship, include your email account to find connections, create a punchy tagline about your passions. By giving you the sense that you haven't finished filling out your profile yet, it insists that you reveal even more information about yourself to the platform's community.

## Autoplay

*Figure 9 Having finished a video, a new video begins by default.*

Autoplay is the default setting on YouTube, Netflix, and Hulu—and it reverses the age-old method of watching video. Now you actually have to stand up and turn off a series of videos or episodes to stop watching. In the past, you had to make an active choice to continue watching video. Removing that natural stopping point has pumped up viewing times and has birthed entirely new styles of consuming video: binge watching and binge racing. Binge watching refers to watching one episode after another without pause. Binge racing takes it up a notch by binge watching all episodes of a series starting the moment of a show's release. Netflix's CEO, Reed Hastings, is so confident in the company's grip on our attention that he was quoted as saying, "We actually compete with sleep...and we're winning!"[33].

---

[33] Gaudette, "Netflix Declares War on Sleep, Its Biggest 'Competitor.'"

## SOCIAL MEDIA: THE BUSINESS

As a business, social media has led a charmed existence. Breaking through previous records for corporate valuation, Facebook and Google race with other tech firms like Apple and Amazon toward the first-ever trillion-dollar valuation[34]. How have they managed to amass so much wealth is so few years? In the case of social media platforms, the answer is advertising. A specific type of advertising, targeted advertising, has allowed Facebook and Google to dominate the digital advertising landscape. To give you a sense of scale, companies spent $72 billion on digital advertising in the United States in 2016[35]. According to my back-of-the-envelope calculation, that comes out to roughly $220 per citizen. Targeted advertising leverages the data social media companies have gleaned from your activities online. As we'll discuss further in Chapter 7, many keep tabs of your activity across the web, not just when you interact with their products. Having lots of data about you allows these firms to differentiate themselves from conventional advertisers—billboards, radio, TV spots, the ads above the urinal. By serving ads in a more relevant context, social platforms can guarantee that the advertiser is getting its product in front of its target customer. Hoping to reach Latina women still living at home who enjoy stand-up comedy? Facebook can help. Trying to get your new aftershave in front of millennial men between the ages of 25 and 34? Google has you covered. By knowing a lot about you, these new advertising gatekeepers have turned our smartphone loops into massive profits.

Twitter, Google, and Facebook (which owns Instagram) are publicly traded companies and regularly report how much

---

[34] Galloway, *The Four.*
[35] "US Digital Ad Spending to Surpass TV This Year - EMarketer."

money comes from advertisers paying to gain access to users' eyeballs. In Q2 of 2017, Twitter sourced 85% of its income from advertisers[36]. Figures for Google and Facebook were 88%[37] and 98%[38], respectively. You are not their customer; advertisers are. Don't get me wrong—you are an important piece of what they do, but unless you start spending less time on their platforms or leave entirely, they are predictably unconcerned. The economics of today's social media environment leads me to believe that while technology companies promised to improve the world, they have failed. Google promised to organize all of the world's information. It turned out that "Google policy is to get right up to the creepy line and not cross it," as its CEO, Eric Schmidt, later said[39]. If only we could all agree on where the creepy line was. On the other hand, Facebook claimed it would connect the world. With *The Wall Street Journal* reporting that chronic loneliness affects 40% of us, up "from 15[%] 30 years ago"[40], Facebook appears to have failed as well. All this said, these companies have undoubtedly forever changed our world. I'm just pointing out that they didn't change it in the way your middle school principal expected you to, when she said she couldn't wait to see how you would change the world.

## SOCIAL MEDIA: THE EFFECTS

We've looked at how social media functions as a habit-forming product and as an advertising business. We'll now turn our attention to its effects on us as individuals. Before I share with you what I've identified as the best and worst effects of social

---

[36] "Q2 2017 Letter to Shareholders."
[37] "Alphabet Announces Second Quarter 2017 Results."
[38] "Facebook Reports Second Quarter 2017 Results."
[39] Taplin, *Move Fast and Break Things.*
[40] Ilardi, "Why Personal Tech Is Depressing."

media, take a moment to identify the benefits and drawbacks of your own social media use.

| BENEFITS | DRAWBACKS |
|---|---|
|  |  |
|  |  |
|  |  |
|  |  |

## Benefits to Using Social Media

- **Sharpened Thinking**

While not exclusively the domain of social networks, there is a benefit to having to turn your thoughts and feelings into prose—even emoji-ridden prose. The process of writing for an audience sharpens our thinking, teasing out internal inconsistencies in our thoughts and arguments[41].

- **Sense of Belonging**

People who engage in social media report a sense of belonging, although researchers point out that this benefit likely comes from communication between users, since passive users experienced lower levels of belonging[42].

[41] Thompson, *Smarter Than You Think*.
[42] McNamee, "How Does Facebook Affect Our Sense of Belonging?"

## - Control

When Sherry Turkle asked young people why they prefer asynchronous messaging technology (e.g., chat, texting, email) so much, they were nearly universal in their response: control. When a text comes in, you have options. You could ignore it, or you could immediately reply, or you could sit on it for a few minutes or days before replying. This gives you time to make sure your response is carefully curated. Comparing this style of communication to face-to-face interaction makes in-person communication daunting. In person, all kinds of unexpected moments occur that may be uncomfortable, awkward, or too revealing. It feels emotionally safer for many people to manage their relationships through text-mediated conversation[43].

## Drawbacks to Using Social Media

## - Superficiality

*Figure 10  This is how my life looked on social media. The day-in, day-out reality was nowhere this good.*

---

[43] Turkle, *Alone Together.*

At the risk of pointing out the obvious, the lives projected on social media platforms tend to be highlight reels of our best moments. You tweet when you reunite with an old friend in a new city. When you are crying into your pillow or throwing up in a public restroom, you don't feel the same urge to document your life.

After receiving my master's degree, my wife and I moved to England for my first teaching post. The job was extremely difficult; the students were terrors, calling me names I had to have translated into American English. I was having the worst year of my life up to that point. I slept poorly (thanks to night sweats and nightmares); drank more than usual; and even had a thought that if a car hit me on my bicycle, I might get out of work for a few days. Then, it happened: in a roundabout, my shoulder crushed a sedan's windshield. With no broken bones, I had no choice but to head to work that Monday. I share all of this to let you know that if you'd looked at my Facebook timeline during that year, I would have looked like I was on the edge of nirvana. I was living abroad, making new friends, traveling Europe during school breaks. There is even a particularly ridiculous photo of a few of my coworkers and me drinking, looking like we are having the time of our lives. The caption read, "This is what happens when teachers get together and shiz gets hella realz!!!"

I experienced this as an observer a couple years later when one of my wife's friends was on Jeopardy. My first thought was, why have I never been on Jeopardy? It didn't matter that I wouldn't be good enough at Jeopardy to appear on the show; I was laser-focused on the fact that someone had done something interesting that I would likely never achieve.

## - Public-Private Blur

Figure 11 When we've already read each other's updates, it can feel like there's nothing to talk about anyway.

For a lot of our connections on social media, we keep up with the latest goings-on by reading friends' posts that show up in our news feeds. Then, when we meet in person, we often don't have that much to talk about. We accept that our friends' posts give us a good idea of what they've been up to lately. The truth is that the posts your friends are sharing are not full descriptions of events. There are things that aren't shared with the wider social network. By giving you a false sense that you know all you need to know about your friends' recent lives, you may neglect to ask them questions that only *you* would ask them. When I share stories with different friends, they always ask different questions, and that is what gives our friendships energy. I have one friend who consistently follows up any argument I make with, "What makes you think that?" I have another friend who always wants to hear an update on my extended family when we get together. Imagine how bland our friendships would become if those friends accepted my social media statuses as what was really going on.

### - Evidentiary Experiences

*Figure 12  Taking photos can actually mean planning experiences around the photo.*

Do you remember when cameras were first added to cell phones? As Randall Munroe pointed out, despite all of us carrying high-definition cameras in our pockets, we've still yet to find a credible Loch Ness monster or yeti[44]. At some point, though, many of our photo habits grew lives of their own. Instead of using the camera to document experiences, we began to plan documentable experiences. The need to provide evidence of fun became more important than the fun itself.

---

[44] Munroe, "Xkcd: Settled."

## - Decreased Wellbeing

Many studies have found a correlation between social media use and depressive symptoms, as well as lowered life satisfaction. Correlational studies demonstrate a link between social media and lowered states of wellbeing. To determine if social media use is actually *causing* diminished wellbeing, you'd have to design an experiment where some people continued using social media normally (the control group), and others were asked to take a break from social media (the experimental group). If the group forced off of social media reported higher levels of life satisfaction and improved emotional lives, you'd demonstrate that social media drives decreased wellbeing, and not the other way around. Fortunately, that study was conducted on more than 1000 Danish participants in 2015. The results support the work of previous studies, which demonstrated that social media use leads to a deterioration of mood and affective wellbeing. The benefits of dropping social media were greatest among heavy users, passive users, and users who tended to envy others[45].

## - Social Engineering

This is going to sound ridiculous, but what if Facebook could influence whether or not you vote in the next election? Or what if they figured out how to change your mood, to make you feel more positively or negatively? The crazy thing is, both of those ridiculous-sounding ideas actually happened[46]. Jaron Lanier, a pioneer of virtual reality, responded to this news in a *New York Times* op-ed, saying, "This is only one early publication about a whole new frontier in the manipulation of people, and Facebook

---

[45] Tromholt, "The Facebook Experiment."
[46] O'Neil, *Weapons of Math Destruction*; Sullivan, "Sheryl Sandberg Not Sorry for Facebook Mood Manipulation Study."

shouldn't be singled out as a villain." He goes on to write, "Now that we know that a social network proprietor can engineer emotions for the multitudes to a slight degree, we need to consider that further research on amplifying that capacity might take place. Stealth emotional manipulation could be channeled to sell things (you suddenly find that you feel better after buying from a particular store, for instance), but it might also be used to exert influence in a multitude of other ways"[47]. Most of the social engineering ability of social media companies comes from the fact that you aren't shown all items available in your news feed at any given moment. As mentioned earlier, *New York Times* tech writer Vindu Goel has pointed out that "when someone logs [into Facebook], there are typically about 1500 items the company could display in that person's news feed, but the service shows only about 300 of them"[48]. Different ways of choosing those 300 items profoundly impact users who view them. Should you suspect that you're being socially engineered, knowingly or via a defective algorithm, it would be extraordinarily difficult to prove. You'd have to collect enormous amounts of data from thousands of users.

- **Social "Tupperwarization"**

Tupperware is a line of food storage products that are not primarily sold in stores; they are only available through individuals who host Tupperware parties to sell the products to their friends. Similarly, we are now inundated with posts by friends raving about that new product or restaurant. Is that endorsement genuine, or did that hashtag get them 20% off?

---

[47] Lanier, "Opinion | Should Facebook Manipulate Users?"
[48] Goel, "Facebook Tinkers With Users' Emotions in News Feed Experiment, Stirring Outcry."

Social media has ushered in a new era of social marketing.

Over the last decade, we've witnessed a massive shift in the way social media and brand promotion function. After hundreds of brands invested in Facebook's platform on the assumption that customers who "liked" their brand would receive branded messaging in their news feed, Facebook changed the platform. Thereafter, brands have to pay for Facebook ads to be sure they are reaching their audience[49]. Whether or not the companies pony up for the ads, they continue to pursue space in your feed via "social engagement." Social engagement is the reason your friend is adding #blissyogadenver to his morning workout photo. By offering discounts to users who post positively about them, brands have found their way back onto our news feeds. We have become brand spokespeople, advocates for all kinds of products and services.

## COMMON ONLINE PERSONAS

Having looked at the ways social media affects us, now you'll look closely at the messages you are sending and receiving through your own social network.

Before we look at your social media messaging, you should be familiar with a few common online personas:

### Observer

This type of user spends large amounts of time passively consuming social media. You may pride yourself on not getting drawn into flame wars and political arguments, but you are always there observing, watching, lurking. The most anyone will

---

[49] Galloway, *The Four.*

ever get out of you is a "like" or a go-to comment like "Cute!"

## Content Producer

These folks are responsible for most of what makes its way into our news feeds. They'll let you know their dog is missing them, they just took a power nap, they love the new grocery store #publixlove, and anything else that occurs to them throughout the day. Their mantra is two-fold: document and share.

## Socializer

This type of user is probably the most coveted by the platforms themselves. These users go out of their way to support people and causes they care about. In return, they receive support from friends, most of whom they have real-world connections with as well.

## Troll

If you've ever read internet comments, you know about trolls. These folks derive a sick pleasure from taking other people down a peg, anonymously. There is no topic that is off limits. Evidence suggests that women take the brunt of this abuse[50].

## Sharer

If you fall into this category, you consider yourself a curator of sorts. You keep up with the latest in current events and find diamonds in the rough that your network would love to get their hands on. You pass great or horrifying links along to your network with a short comment to give a hint to your own

---

[50] Pullen, "Yes, Men Can Be Victims of Online Harassment. But in Reality, Women Have It Much Worse."

admiration or outrage of the piece.

## Avatar Architect

This type of user describes a diverse group that is working hard to show how pretty, powerful, or promotable they are. Everything they post or comment supports a particular, personal brand they have often spent years curating.

…

Here comes the scary part. I'd like you to open your favorite social media platform and find a list of your recent posts. What are your posts like? What signals are they sending to other users?

## List any themes you recognize in your own posts.

**1.**

**2.**

**3.**

Now hop into the news feed section of the platform, where you'll see content generated by the folks you follow. What are their posts like? What signals are they sending you?

## List any themes you recognize in others' posts.

**1.**

**2.**

**3.**

My suspicion is that you didn't discover anything you didn't already know deep down, but that you did notice a gulf between who we aspire to be and who we actually are. Being inauthentic comes with the online territory[51].

At this point, you may be wondering just how much time you're spending on social media. To answer that question, you need to go no further than your RescueTime or Moment data.

The table below should make it easy to calculate the number of days per year you'll spend on any particular app if current trends persist.

| APP | TIME SPENT PER DAY (MINUTES) | | DAYS PER YEAR |
|---|---|---|---|
| Instagram | 60 | × 0.2535 = | 15.21 |
| | | × 0.2535 = | |
| | | × 0.2535 = | |
| | | × 0.2535 = | |
| | | × 0.2535 = | |
| **Total Time Spent on Smartphone** | | | |
| All Apps | | × 0.2535 = | |

---

51 Turkle, *Alone Together*.

## HAPPY MEDIUM

In this section, I'll present several ways to reduce the time you spend passively consuming social content. While I don't want you to think there is a single fix that will help everyone, I will encourage you to be ruthless. Distracting apps are re-installable, should you change your mind. More likely, the deeper you cut down your social media activity, the happier you'll be and the more connected you'll feel to people in person.

### Deactivating Accounts

You don't need Facebook, Instagram, Twitter, LinkedIn, Reddit, Google+, YouTube, *and* SnapChat. Pick one or two social media platforms, and deactivate your other accounts.

### Shifting to the Browser

Delete every social media app off of your phone. Please do this. I'm asking in the way that someone who has been to an indoor skydiving place describes his own experience. Rather than continue telling you about it, we just need to get you in the massive air tunnel. You'll never be the same afterward. Go ahead and remove the apps. If you do want to use the one or two accounts you still have active, do so from a desktop or laptop browser. That will at least make sure you aren't on your phone while driving or during meals.

## AppDetox (Android)

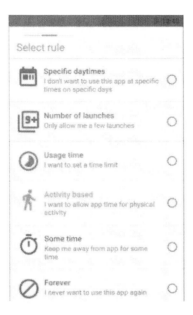

*Figure 13  Keep yourself accountable to limits you set for your app usage.*

play.google.com/store/apps/details?id=de.dfki.appdetox

This is an app you can install on your Android devices. It allows you to limit your access to particular apps at particular times. If you are wasting your weekends on Instagram, you can prevent yourself from using Instagram on Saturdays and Sundays without affecting your weekdays. Maybe Twitter is keeping you up at night, so you lock yourself out after 6 p.m.

## Restrictions (iOS)

This built-in iOS feature allows you to set a passcode that prevents you from using an app you have installed. You can also set it to prevent installing any new apps, in case you are tempted to replace your LinkedIn fix with Twitter. Although initially introduced to keep your toddler from paying your water bill, this feature works well if you ask a trusted friend to lock you out of your own permissiveness.

## Chrome Extensions

Chances are high that you use Chrome when you browse the internet—60%, to be exact[52]. Chrome becomes the window through which you access the internet. It manages cookies and caching, and other things that you probably want to know nothing about. Over the years, software engineers have come up with creative ways to add new functionality to the Chrome browser. These are called Chrome extensions and are easily installed (one click) via the Chrome Web Store. If you aren't on Chrome, not to fear, most browsers have similar extensions available, sometimes called plug-ins. Unfortunately, Chrome extensions do not work on smartphones.

---

[52] "Browser Market Share."

## - ScrollStopper

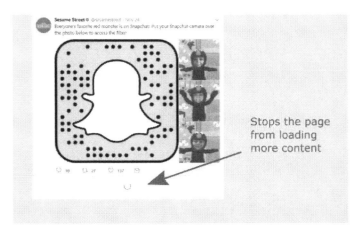

*Figure 14 ScrollStopper prevents more content from loading on several social platforms.*

chrome.google.com/webstore/detail/scrollstopper/pbadlbgcb kmhdlnbancbdmimccdkhnoe

I created this extension myself, so I can't truly give you an objective review. The power of ScrollStopper is that it takes popular platforms (Facebook, Instagram, LinkedIn, Twitter, Pinterest, Reddit, and BuzzFeed) and removes the infinite scroll feature from their feeds. For instance, when you log on to LinkedIn, you'll see eight or 10 stories but no more. This means you can stop by your favorite social network for a few minutes without investing an unknown amount of time scrolling.

- **Nanny for Google Chrome**

| Blocked URLs | Whitelisted URLs | Tags | General Options | LockDown | Validate Req |
|---|---|---|---|---|---|

**DETAILS OF URLS TO BLOCK**

| Block Set Name * | Social Media |
|---|---|
| URLs * | www.facebook.com<br>www.twitter.com<br>www.youtube.com<br>www.instagram.com<br>www.reddit.com |
| Block Time * | 0900-1700 |
| Max Time : | 30    minutes for every  1 Day (24 hours)  ▼ |
| Apply On Days * | ☐ Sunday ☑ Monday ☑ Tuesday ☑ Wednesday ☑ Thursday ☑ Friday ☐ Saturday |
| Tags | ▼  Add Tag |
| Added Tags | |

  Save URL    Clear Tags    Clear All Fields

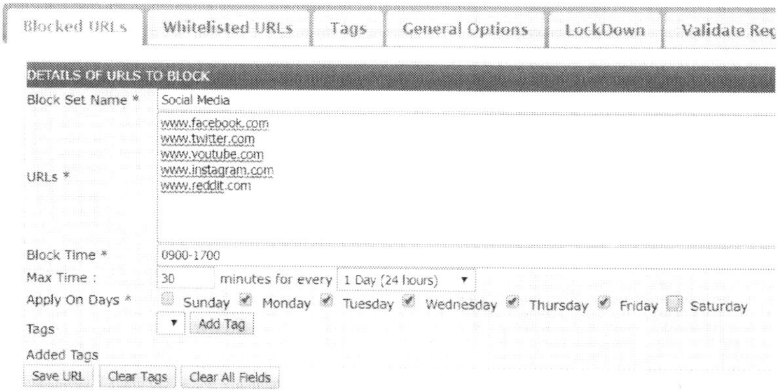

*Figure 15  Set custom rules for your browsing.*

chrome.google.com/webstore/detail/nanny-for-google-chrome-t/cljcgchbnolheggdgaeclffeagnnmhno

This Chrome extension allows your intentional self to smack some sense into your tired, weak-willed, future self. You can configure the settings to limit your exposure to any group(s) of sites. Doing so allows you to do interesting things like use social media or news sites for no more than 30 minutes between 9 a.m. and 5 p.m. Once you go over your limit, Nanny shuts you down, replacing the offending site with the admonition, "Shouldn't you be working?"

# SET YOUR GOALS

We've looked closely at how social media operates on a high level as well as on a personal level. I've given you some ideas about how to limit your smartphone loop, so the time has come to commit yourself to a social media goal.

**If I do not meet my goal, I will give $\_\_\_\_ to _____.**

**My goal:**

If you are having trouble coming up with a goal specific to social media, here are a few of my favorite suggestions:

- Deactivate all but one or two social media accounts.

- Remove all social media apps from your phone.

- Install ScrollStopper to limit time spent on social media.

- Set limits on social media with Nanny for Google Chrome.

- Let your SnapStreaks reset to 0.

In the next chapter, we'll attempt to replace our frantic, headless-chicken multitasking with focused productivity. Foraging theory will help us understand our built-in weaknesses and identify easy ways to decrease our distractibility. I'll provide plenty of practical suggestions for how to set up an environment where focused, deep work will flourish. Finally, we'll briefly look at a few ways to ward off email distractions as we close the chapter.

# FOUR

## FOCUS: The Art of Monotasking

*The art of being wise is the art of knowing what to overlook.*

WILLIAM JAMES

In the last chapter, we looked in detail at social media, examining the ways it has seduced us into compulsively checking platforms for the newest, most provocative content. Now, we will get a little "meta" and will turn our attention to our own attention. The ability to sustain your attention will pay off big when you have important work to get done. Work worth doing deserves your full attention. By thoroughly examining multitasking's allure and pitfalls, we'll unearth work styles and tools that support extended periods of deep work.

To start off, I'd like you to take a moment to complete a focusing meditation. If you've never meditated before, not to fear; this is about as simple as meditations come. In Chapter 9, I'll go into more detail about a secular form of meditation called mindfulness. For now, all I want you to do is to find a comfortable seated position with your back straight. You will close your eyes and take a few deep breaths. As you breathe, notice where you feel the air coming into and out of your body.

Once you've identified a particular spot (common choices include your nasal passages, your top lip, your throat, or belly), spend five to 10 minutes breathing deeply, maintaining your focus on the feel of the air drifting in and out of your body. If you become distracted, simply and without judgment take your focus back to the spot you are focusing on and begin again.

**In the area below, describe your experience. Did you become distracted? What drew your focus away from your point of concentration? Were you able to maintain your concentration for any extended periods?**

My guess is that you became distracted at least a few times during your meditation. Everybody does. We all have daily frustrations, stories we tell ourselves, undone to-dos, and many more thoughts that butt in whenever they sense a moment of peace and calm. With this brief exercise, I hope you noticed just how complicated maintaining your focus can be, even when you're being very intentional about it. It's no surprise that we end up multitasking when we work!

## MULTITASKING

Have you ever been asked in a job interview about your greatest weakness? For a long time, my go-to answer was an inability to multitask. When I answered this question, I was looking for a strength I could dress up as a weakness. I'd read several articles suggesting that aside from tasks that become automatic like chewing gum and walking, multitasking was not actually possible. To be honest, not being a proficient multitasker was another way of saying, "Sometimes I will get too engrossed in my assignments." I'm not sure this response ever came off well; humble brags tend to attract eye rolls.

Nevertheless, research shows that in reality *no one* can really multitask; it's just not how the human brain works. What we call "multitasking" is really our minds rapidly switching focus between a bunch of different tasks (and not, as we may imagine, performing them all at once)[53]. Multitasking seems efficient—which is why we do it—but let's examine this presumption a little closer with a practical example.

For this activity, find a timer and follow the directions for each exercise below.

---

[53] Goldhill, "Multitasking Is Scientifically Impossible, so Give up Now."

## Exercise A

Set your timer for one minute. During that minute, focus on listing as many states as possible in the column on the left. Once one minute is up, switch to the right column and spend one minute listing as many TV shows as you can think of.

| STATES | TV SHOWS |
| --- | --- |
|  |  |

## Exercise B

Great work. Now, set your timer for two minutes. This time, only spend 15 seconds working in the left column of the chart below before switching to the right column; then switch back to the left column after 15 seconds. Alternate between the two columns every 15 seconds until the two minutes are up.

| COUNTRIES | ANIMALS |
|---|---|
| | |

As you may have already figured out, Exercise A demonstrates monotasking (focusing on completing one task before moving on to another), while Exercise B showcases the attentional whiplash you experience as you try to multitask (that is, do multiple things at once).

**Having completed both charts, what are your observations?**

**What feelings did you experience as you were switching more frequently?**

**Which exercise had better outcomes, and which one felt more efficient?**

When I've done this activity with groups, a couple of themes tend to emerge. The first thing most people say is that switching lists every 15 seconds is frustrating. Many people let out loud sighs or scrunch up their faces with disgust when asked to switch yet again.

The other thing you may have noticed is that your ideas come to you in bursts. This is because you are pulling information from your deep-storage memory up to your short-term memory. So, for example, if you put Mississippi on the states list, you are likely to list several other Southern states before you get to Rhode Island, which you would probably only list once you focus your efforts on states in New England.

To demonstrate this concept further, answer the following question.

### What did you have for dinner last Friday?

First off, that question is a doozy for many folks, myself included. Whether or not you came up with the answer, the point is this: In order to figure out what you ate for dinner last Friday, you have to build up some context for last Friday night's dinner. To do so, you trace out as many details surrounding the dinner as possible. Were you around other people last Friday? Where were you eating last Friday? What do Fridays normally look like for you?

Once you start to get some details in place and you've built a decent mental picture of last Friday night, it becomes easy enough to pluck out the particular fact you want. If I stayed on the topic of Friday night and followed up with another question—something like, "What did you do after dinner?"— you could easily come up with it. But if I switched to a new topic and asked, "Where were you at dinnertime last Tuesday?" it is back to the drawing board. Your mental picture of last Friday is worthless in this context, so you'll have to build up a new context, one for last Tuesday evening.

I share these examples to make it clear that every time we attempt a task, our brains must first contextualize that task before we can perform it. When we monotask, our brains only have to do the context prep-work once. In contrast, when we multitask, our brains have to do this work over and over every time we switch back and forth between tasks. This repeated (and ultimately inefficient) context work was why you might have found Exercise B to be rather frustrating.

Here's another way to look at how context operates when we multitask. First, let's examine an ideal situation in which we minimize time spent building context for the tasks we have to complete. In other words, each task's context would be built one time only. Once you loaded the context for the first task, you would complete the entire task without interruption and then move on to building context for your second task, which you would also complete without interruption. If we visually represented that scenario, it would look something like this:

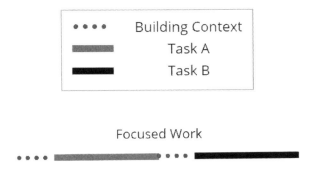

*Figure 16  Context is only built once for each task.*

Now, imagine what actually happens. More likely, you would build context for your first task and begin. A short time later, you'd be interrupted by a new task, your second task. You'd have to build context for it before beginning. Then you might remember your first task needs to be finished, so you go back to it. Here you'd need to build the context for your first task again before completing it. With the first task finally complete, you'll need to build context again for your second task before finishing it. (If all of that sounds confusing, it's for good reason!) This switching-back-and-forth scenario would look something like this:

## Distracted Work

*Figure 17  Context must be built multiple times for each task.*

Notice that your actual time spent on each task is similar in both examples, but the total time to complete both tasks is different—the line in the distracted, multitasked example is much longer. That's because you had to build context for your tasks twice as many times.

Why would we multitask if it is so much less efficient? Unfortunately, multitasking tricks us into thinking we are getting more done than we actually are. Multitasking also helps beat back the boredom that our less engaging tasks bring forth. Gloria Mark from the University of California Irvine has been studying work environments for decades and points out other downsides to multitasking. She's found that people who multitask often end up working faster to compensate for time lost to building context over and over. However, she warns, "Working faster with interruptions has its cost: people in the interrupted conditions experienced a higher workload, more stress, higher frustrations, more time pressure, and effort. So interrupted work may be done faster but at a price"[54].

We've all had that moment of standing up after an hour online with no clue what we did or where our time went. Evidence suggests that our time online is often scattered as we yank our attention from page to page or app to app. Most web pages are viewed for 10 seconds or less[55]. In 2012, we were only averaging one minute per app session on our smartphones[56]. Why are we so distraction-prone online?

## FORAGING

Somewhat strangely, we can get some answers by looking at research done with foraging creatures like chipmunks. When chipmunks are collecting nuts, they need to optimize the time they spend at each source (tree). They want to optimize in part to conserve their energy and to be the healthiest—and therefore sexiest—chipmunks around when it comes time to mate, but they also want to avoid traveling for too long in the open. Hawks and owls are all too happy to snatch up chipmunks caught between trees. Those factors have made chipmunks very good at figuring out the best amount of time to spend at each tree before moving on. Chipmunk behavior is consistent enough to be observed by scientists, who have figured out the two main factors that affect how long chipmunks stay at one tree before heading to the next one.

First, the distance between the trees makes a big difference. If your current tree still has nuts and it is a long, scary trip to your next tree, you tend to stay at each tree longer. On the other hand,

---

[54] Gazzaley and Rosen, *The Distracted Mind.*
[55] Carr, *The Shallows.*
[56] Eler, "Study."

if trees are close together, the trip isn't so scary and you can always go back to the first tree if the next one is a dud.

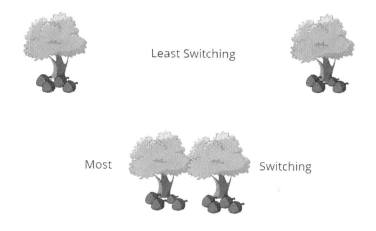

Figure 18 *When the distance between trees is farther, chipmunks stay longer at each tree.*

The other factor that influences time spent at each tree is the nut density. At the risk of pointing out the obvious, chipmunks stay longer at trees with lots of nuts. Why leave a place where food is plentiful? On the flip side, if nuts are sparse, you spend so much time looking for the next nut that you reach a point when it's worth braving the trail to your next tree in hopes of better luck.

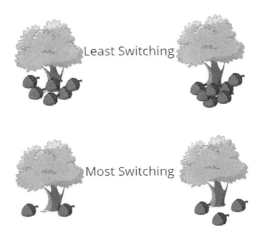

*Figure 19  When trees have dense nuts, chipmunks stay longer at each tree.*

Distance and density are powerful forces for determining how long any foraging creature spends at a food source[57]. If we were to combine these two factors to create an environment where chipmunks would switch trees as little as possible, we could do so by placing trees packed densely with nuts at large distances from one another. To achieve the opposite—to create an environment where chipmunks switched very frequently— placing trees with sparse nuts close together would do the trick.

---

[57] Gazzaley and Rosen, *The Distracted Mind.*

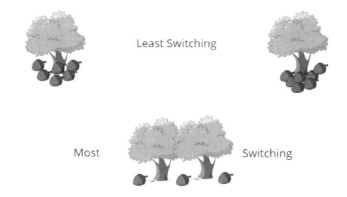

Least Switching

Most          Switching

*Figure 20  Chipmunks switch least when nuts are densely packed under trees that are far apart.*

Humans searching for information on electronic devices have these same tendencies[58]. For comparison's sake, imagine that we're the chipmunks, information is the "nuts" we're foraging for, and different websites are our "trees" or sources.

Now think about how your browser and smartphone work. "Distances" between information sources online are tiny. Browser page load times are measured in milliseconds, and jumping from one app to another on your phone is nearly instantaneous.

How about density? Compared to past media (e.g., books, magazines, newspapers), information online and in apps is low in density. Platforms like Twitter, Facebook, LinkedIn, Snapchat, even blogs, encourage us to post our thoughts, but please keep them brief. Think about how small the box where you type your post is, and recall that long posts are truncated

---

[58] Gazzaley and Rosen.

with a "Read More" link, maintaining the illusion of brevity. It's all purposely designed to keep the information density low.

We've created an environment on the internet that optimizes for the least amount of time at each information source (short distance, low density). For a chipmunk, the equivalent would be trees with very sparse nuts bunched closely together. A foraging chipmunk in this environment would run rapidly from tree to tree, never staying long in one spot. Next time you find yourself experiencing web whiplash, flitting from site to site as fast as you can click, now you know why.

The majority of our digital tools were built with little thought for whether they work well for humans. Even much of the work that user-experience designers do boils down to simplifying processes so that a higher percentage of customers will cross some finish line, whether it's filling in profiles or completing payment for items in their shopping carts. So far there has been little attention devoted to making the internet a better environment for our mental energies. When we bounce around from site to site, app to app, like a chipmunk racing from tree to tree, it's tiring, whether we realize it or not.

Nicholas Carr describes this current state of digital overwhelm not as "information overload" so much as "ambient overload." The metaphor he draws on is the old needle-in-a-haystack image. "Ambient overload," he explains, "doesn't involve needles in haystacks. It involves haystack-sized piles of needles." In other words, when the whole haystack is full of what we're looking for, the effect is downright painful. When we experience ambient overload, "we're surrounded by so much information that is of immediate interest to us that we feel overwhelmed by the never-ending pressure of trying to keep up with it all." And we know too well what happens next: "We keep clicking links, keep hitting the refresh key, keep opening new tabs, keep checking email inboxes and social media feeds, keep scanning Amazon and Netflix recommendations—and yet the pile of interesting information never shrinks"[59].

If you're feeling overwhelmed just reading about it, take a deep breath and read on. There are lots of ways to mitigate our natural inclination to flit from thing to thing. We'll cover those techniques in the next section, which delves into the subtle art of monotasking.

## MONOTASKING

By now, you realize we're going to need a plan if we are going to combat our natural tendency to multitask. To begin, imagine you are a chipmunk and you are trying to find ways to increase your time per tree. If this chipmunk is bright and had a brainstorming session with other chipmunks where there were no bad ideas, some of these thoughts might come up:

*1. Make nuts taste better at your current tree.*

*2. Cut down nearby nut trees.*

*3. Spray a chemical on nearby trees' nuts to make them taste bad.*

Thinking about chipmunks brainstorming in a boardroom—mine were wearing pantsuits while sipping Fiji water—is a lot of fun, but how could this operate in a human context? If we translated those chipmunk ideas into advice for information-hungry humans, it would look something like this:

---

[59] Carr, *Utopia Is Creepy*.

*1. Make a boring task more engaging.*

For example, listening to soft music while completing mundane work is a great way to keep working for longer periods.

*2. Increase the distance between your current task and other tasks.*

Remove all the piles on your desk from arm's reach[60]. Keep your smartphone in your backpack instead of your pocket.

*3. Decrease the desirability of distractions.*

One way is to configure your phone's lock screen so it won't show you a text's sender or message.

...

Remember, be ruthless with your environment, but be compassionate towards yourself. Up next, I'll give you a few more tips for monotasking.

## The Pomodoro Technique

*Figure 21 Use a sand timer for an enhanced Pomodoro Technique experience.*

---

[60] Carnegie, *How To Enjoy Your Life And Your Job.*

The Pomodoro Technique was created when Italian Francesco Cirillo started using a kitchen timer, shaped like a tomato—"pomodoro" in Italian—to work in 25-minute bursts. After each 25-minute work session, the Pomodoro Technique prescribes a five-minute break. The cycle is then repeated, 25 minutes of work followed by five-minute breaks, until four cycles have been completed. At that point, you take a longer, 15- to 30-minute extended break[61]. I've tried using this technique many times. Each time my experience was the same. I'd become unbelievably productive. The sense of time scarcity, combined with the knowledge that I could deal with interruptions and distractions in my next break, led to a lot of work getting done. The only problem was that it never felt sustainable. I couldn't keep to the technique after three or four cycles. The main issue was that using a kitchen timer or digital timer (search the Chrome Web Store for Pomodoro Timer, and you'll find plenty) became infuriating. I'd be deep in important work, and then all of a sudden, DING BEEP BUZZ. I'm being interrupted by the timer and told now it is time to take a break. Hopefully the timer didn't hit anyone on its flight out of my window.

Fortunately, I've recently made peace with Pomodoro by using a sand timer. I found a half-hour sand timer on eBay for eight bucks. Now I use the sand timer to time my Pomodoros. The advantage is that it does not beep. It does, however, run out of sand. Moments when I look up and notice that it's run out of sand tend to be moments when I am in need of a break and am scanning for distractions. By using my sand timer version of the Pomodoro Technique, I've been able to build breaks into my day without interrupting myself unnecessarily.

---

[61] Cirillo, "The Pomodoro Technique®."

## Identification of Avocado Tasks

Have you ever noticed that avocados can be fairly silverware-intensive? To eat an avocado, you need a knife to cut it open. After that, you'll need a spoon to scoop the flesh out of the skin. Finally, you mash the avocado flesh with a fork before you are ready to eat it. Few fruits or vegetables are such heavy silverware users. In the same way, we all have items on our to-do lists that act like avocados. I'm not talking about simple to-dos like "buy new shoes." You could do that while waiting on a delayed flight, lounging on your couch, even on an extended trip to the toilet—don't do that, but you could. Avocado tasks have multiple moving parts. Think about a task like "schedule kayaking trip." In order to schedule a kayaking trip, you'll need to sync up schedules with your friends and potentially a significant other before you can choose a date. Once you choose a date, there are other tasks that will spawn out of that parent task. Things like "pack bag," "buy snacks," and "choose location" will all have to be done once the date is nailed down. Identifying to-do items that are hiding other subtasks will help you prioritize your tasks effectively and budget time appropriately.

## Task Batching

Think about your email inbox for a moment. At first glance, your emails may seem fairly diverse, and they may be. But the process you go through to deal with each email is likely similar. You need to view any attachments and then prepare a response. Because the process is the same, I recommend knocking all of your emails out in a single stretch. Once you are in the email zone, each email takes less time to deal with. If you ever bake, you've probably already done this type of thing before. Whenever I make banana bread, I double the recipe. I'm going to have to get flour, sugar, oil, milk, eggs, bananas, vanilla, and nuts out, mix them together, and bake. For nearly the same amount of effort, I can have twice as much banana bread. In the same way, by batching tasks with similar processes, you'll spend less time processing and more time celebrating your beautiful "inbox zero."

## Do Not Disturb

This is a feature that comes baked into both Android and iOS devices. Do Not Disturb manages the times when you don't want to be interrupted by your phone. You can use it manually, switching it on at the movie theater, for example. Or you can put it on a schedule. I use this feature to protect my sleep. From 9:30 p.m. to 6 a.m. the following day, calls and texts don't make their usual dings, lights, or vibrations. If you are hesitant to adopt this feature because you want to make yourself available to family members 24/7, I have great news. The feature includes support for allowing favorite contacts to reach you even during Do Not Disturb time. It can also be set to allow repeated callers through, which means if there's an emergency and someone calls you over and over in a short amount of time, you can still get the call.

## Nanny for Google Chrome

I've mentioned this Chrome extension before, in the context of limiting the time you spend on social media. I've added it here as well to remind you of its flexibility in setting some guardrails on your focus. If you are self-interrupting by obsessively checking the news, set a limit on how much time you give to current events.

## Cold Turkey

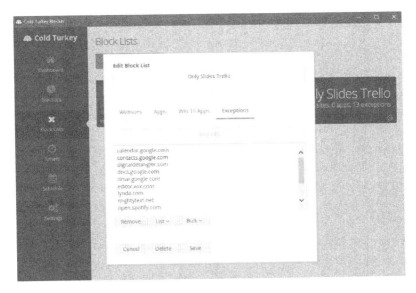

*Figure 22  Cold Turkey lets you block yourself from as much or as little of the web as you'd like.*

getcoldturkey.com

Cold Turkey is a powerful tool. It installs directly to your desktop or laptop. Once you've installed it, you can whitelist or blacklist particular sites. Whitelisting a site refers to configuring software to allow you to visit that site. Blacklisting is the opposite, specifying which sites you won't be able to access. For serious productivity, blacklist all sites and then whitelist only sites that are absolutely necessary for your work. If you buy the paid version of Cold Turkey, you can blacklist and whitelist sites on a schedule. Jack Reeves of Homescreen Zero recommended that approach to me; now all of my internet-based work takes place after noon, when Cold Turkey turns the rest of the internet back on.

## EMAIL

I remember a dinner several years ago when a friend and his wife lamented the rise of email. Their main complaints were:

*Too many emails*

*Never-ending exchanges*

*Copying other people on emails, which creates additional pressure (if you've ever had a request copied to your manager, you understand this one)*

*The imposition of receiving an email*

I agree with all of those complaints, but as easy as it is to hate email, it appears to be here to stay. My cardinal rules for determining if emails are worth your time are as follows:

### Emails from Humans ✔

When another human takes time to send you something, it is courteous to acknowledge the email with a reply.

### Emails from Machines ✘

If someone commented on your comment on someone else's comment about the link your friend Andy shared, you don't need to get an email about it. Same goes for any email that is automatically generated. The possible exception to this rule would be newsletters or listservs you enjoy reading. Be judicious, though; if you haven't had time to read the content lately or if people are overusing the email list, shut it down.

## Emails on Smartphones ✖

Having email on your smartphone can allow you to know about something a bit earlier than if you waited until you got to your inbox on your laptop. This is another instance where we've been trained by variable rewards to compulsively tend to our email. If you doubt that you could get by without email on your phone, think back to a time when getting an email on your phone made a meaningful difference to your response. Chances are, your example is something like, "I found out about [insert big news] a half hour earlier than I would have otherwise." In cases of true emergency, someone will call or text, not email.

Now that the sermon is over, I have a couple of practical tips for managing your inbox. Both of these suggestions are Gmail-specific, but you may be able to find similar options with other email providers.

## Filter Messages Like These

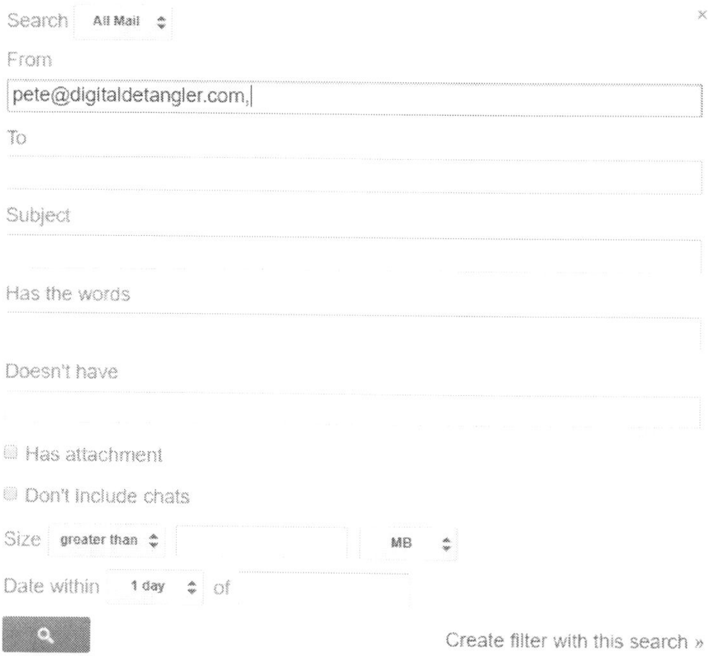

*Figure 23  Gmail's search box allows the creation of a custom email filter.*

When you are looking at a particular email and have decided that you no longer want to receive similar emails, select "Filter Messages Like These" from the drop-down above the email. There is no shortage of options, but most often simply "skipping the inbox" and automatically archiving future emails from the same sender does the job. This comes in handy when you're having trouble unsubscribing from bulk emails or when you can't find an easy way to unsubscribe.

## Inbox When Ready for Gmail

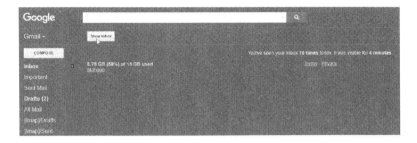

*Figure 24  My inbox is hidden by default.*

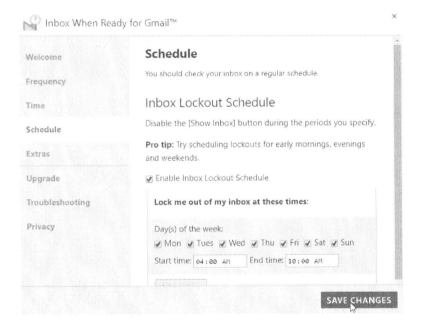

*Figure 25  Options allow you to block yourself out of your inbox on a
specified schedule.*

inboxwhenready.org

Inbox When Ready is a Chrome extension that has the potential to fundamentally change your relationship with email. It hides your inbox by default, replacing it with a small button. If you want to see your inbox, you have to click the button to show your inbox. Having to manually opt in to seeing your inbox means you're less likely to log in to your email to send something, only to lose yourself digging through your inbox, having forgotten about the original email you intended to send. Without your inbox shown, your email page becomes more of a tool and less of a distraction. Another great feature of Inbox When Ready is the ability to lock yourself out of your inbox on a schedule. You can use this feature to protect your most productive hours from becoming time you spend on email. Without inbox access, you still can send emails and can look up specific past emails or attachments, all without the impulse to inspect your inbox. You also can set limits on how many times each day you can access your inbox. This tool is for folks who don't trust themselves near an inbox and are ready to set real limits on their email habit.

...

In the past two chapters, we've taken a moment to set a goal or intention. If you are like many folks, you're probably struggling to kick the deep-seated compulsion to check your phone over and over. It is important to acknowledge that the journey you are on is not easy nor is it straightforward. There will be a lot of frustrations, and you may feel like you are taking one step forward and two steps back. That is okay. As you form new habits, the old ones will wear off. In the meantime, be wary of any digital activities you may be using to replace your old habits.

Take another look at your RescueTime or Moment data and see if you notice anything. Has your mobile gaming grown since you deleted Instagram? Are you finding news sites irresistible since you gave up email? If so, you aren't the first to experience this phenomenon of compensation.

Back in the early- to mid-20th century, something unusual happened. During the same time that labor-saving devices like electric washers, automatic washers, automatic dryers, and wash-and-wear clothing were being introduced, the amount of time per week Americans spent doing laundry stayed the same, hovering around six hours. How could that be? As laundry became easier to do, rather than spending less time doing it, hygiene standards rose; the entire country decided that clothes needed to be washed more often[62]. I share that anecdote to illustrate our impulse to compensate, in curious ways, for time saved. As you begin to retrain yourself toward different activities, beware that you could compensate for old habits with new habits. Make sure the new habits move you toward your goals and don't simply substitute one bad habit for another.

---

[62] Schor, *The Overworked American.*

# SET YOUR GOALS

I've given you some ideas about how to set yourself up for sustained focus, and the time has come to commit yourself to a goal.

**If I do not meet my goal, I will give $____ to _____.**

**My goal:**


Having trouble coming up with an attention-specific goal? Here are a few suggestions:

- Set up Nanny for Google Chrome for three distracting sites.

- Schedule smartphone Do Not Disturb.

- Remove email app from smartphone.

- Schedule emails with Inbox When Ready for Gmail.

- Limit internet access with Cold Turkey to create space for deep work.

- Use the Pomodoro Technique to start your day.

Coming up, we'll explore tools and hot-keys that will elevate your technology game, making you a full-fledged power user. Spend more time crushing work and less time moving your mouse to the top of the application to click the tiny X. Learning new habits, especially keyboard habits, can have a steep learning curve, but practice makes perfect—and time saved on the keyboard pays dividends for the rest of your life.

# FIVE

## CLARIFY: Pairing Tools with Tasks

*There is nothing quite so useless as doing with great efficiency something that should not be done at all.*

PETER DRUCKER

One of the best ways to save large amounts of time is to take a hard look at tasks you perform repetitively and then to investigate a few factors. Think about the number of times you perform the task in a given time period (n), the time it normally takes ($t_{normal}$), and the time it would take with an improved process ($t_{improved}$). Your time saved ($t_{saved}$) is then a simple calculation:

$$t_{saved} = n \times (t_{normal} - t_{improved})$$

Looking at the formula, you can start to identify the different factors that influence how much time you save. For example, let's think through closing an application on your laptop. The more you close applications, the more time you will save if you find a way to close applications quicker. The bigger the difference between your normal time and the improved time, the more time you save. In the case of closing applications, your normal time may be a couple of seconds; you have to move your mouse up to the top right part of the screen and click on the X icon. If you learn the keyboard shortcut (discussed later this chapter) that allows you to close the application using a simple hot-key, your improved time may drop to a fraction of a second, say 0.5 seconds. Saving one and a half seconds each time you close an application may seem like small potatoes, but consider that you keep saving a second and a half, multiple times a day, *for the rest of your life.* I share this example at the beginning of the power-user chapter because the information in this chapter has the potential to completely change the way you interact with your laptop. It could save you minutes every day and put you into a mind-meld with your computer in the way that only tool-wielding primates can understand.

I've brought together a group of the easiest-to-learn, biggest-payoff hacks for making the most of your laptop, and we'll explore them in this chapter. If this is too much too quickly, work on one new technique each week. I've found that late afternoon is a great time to learn new hot-keys and tools. You're generally not super productive at the end of your day, and your brain is ready to explore anything more engaging than that stack of TPS reports.

Before I launch into the tools and hot-keys that you'll learn, I want to address a couple of concerns you might have at this point.

### I'm confused...I thought this book was about using technology less.

I sympathize with your confusion. This is a great time to come clean. I use technology all the time, and much of it I love. So, if some screen time is considered okay and some is wasteful, how do you decide which is which? Nicholas Carr has written on this subject for decades and suggests we make the distinction as follows: tools are good, and passive media consumption is bad[63]. Tools expand our world, allowing us to do new, interesting work that wouldn't have been possible if we were still washing our clothes by hand and churning butter in one of those cool cylindrical contraptions. Consuming media—whether that means watching television, viewing YouTube videos, or scrolling our news feeds—tends to shrink our worlds. At best, it relaxes us. At worst, it draws us into unhealthy comparisons and keeps us still for long enough to endanger our health. Our bodies didn't evolve with access to 24/7 stimulation, so we are susceptible to being hijacked by the carousel of entertainment beckoning us to watch just a little longer. My hope is that by teaching you more about how to efficiently use your laptop, you'll have more time to create incredible products and services, or to take a walk outside, or to connect in person with others.

### I like the way I do things. I'm not interested in learning about ways to speed up my workflow.

I've definitely run into this before. My first response is that I hope you give this a fair shot. Consider for a moment if you applied the same logic to your daily commute. If you moved to a new city and it took you 45 minutes of winding on back roads to arrive at your office and then a coworker told you about a better route, one that would save you 15 minutes each way, would your response really be, "I like the way I'm getting here"? My guess is that you'd try the new way and love it. A few mornings a week, you might turn on mental autopilot and find yourself taking the slow way again by accident—but whenever

---

[63] Carr, *Utopia Is Creepy.*

you could, you'd save yourself that half hour. With an extra half hour of every work day for the next few years, you could learn to play the violin, cook dinner from scratch, brew your own beer, or just stare at the wall. The point is, you'd probably rather do any of those activities than sit in your car on a congested road.

## TOOLING UP

In this section, I'll introduce several tools that may need to be installed before you can use them, depending on whether you are a Windows or Apple user.

### Clipboard Manager

If you spend a lot of time cutting and pasting, clipboard managers are a lifesaver. Your laptop's clipboard comes with one spot by default. By that I mean if you cut "A" and then cut "B," "A" is no longer available. There's no way to get it back. This can make working with your clipboard risky at times, if you are copying and pasting important information. A clipboard manager solves this issue by expanding your clipboard to keep many of the things you cut or copied in the past. You can go back to about 100 old items that on a standard clipboard would have been long gone.

Windows: Ditto (ditto-cp.sourceforge.net)

Mac: Flycut (itunes.apple.com/us/app/flycut-clipboard-manager/id442160987)

### Window Manager

Getting application windows to take up a particular side of the screen becomes a cinch when you access window management capabilities. On Windows, this is as simple at holding down the Windows key and pressing direction arrows until the window is sized and placed appropriately. On a Mac, to achieve the same end, I recommend a free tool called Spectacle. It has a number of capabilities that make it a dream to use, including allowing you to reconfigure which keys you use to activate it.

Windows: Windows key + [any direction arrow]

Mac: Spectacle (spectacleapp.com)

## Application Launcher

When you are ready to open an application, you need to be able to do so quickly. Windows comes with this ability, but many users don't know about it. All you have to do is hit (don't hold) the Windows key, and then begin typing the name of the application you want to open. Once it appears, hit enter, and the application will open. On a Mac, the same effect can be achieved through the Spotlight feature, but I love a little application called Alfred. It does many of the same things as Spotlight but can also lock, restart, or shut down your laptop.

Windows: Windows key + [type application name]

Mac: Alfred (alfredapp.com)

## Caps Lock to Ctrl

The Caps Lock key is totally whack. This thing is sitting on prime keyboard real estate and is used once every six months. Many of the hot-keys we'll explore in the next section use the Ctrl key in combination with other keys. Wouldn't it make more sense if you could turn your Caps Lock key into another Ctrl key? You can do so on both Windows and Mac fairly easily.

Windows machines will need to install a small tool called Sharpkeys. If you use a Mac, it is even easier—go into your keyboard settings and adjust your "Modifier Keys."

Windows: Sharpkeys (sharpkeys.en.softonic.com)

Mac: In keyboard settings, change Modifier Keys.

## THE HOT-KEYS

Now that you've souped up your machine, you are ready to learn the hot-keys and level-up your skills.

### Open an Application

Windows: Press Windows key once, begin to type application name, press enter once the application name appears.

Mac: Activate Alfred or Spotlight, begin to type application, press enter once the application name appears.

### Close an Application

Windows: Hold Alt while you press F4.

Mac: Hold Cmd while you press q.

### Mini-Close an Application

Allow me to explain. In a number of applications, you might want to close part of the application without closing the entire application. Think of a browser with many tabs or one of seven PDF documents open. If you used the hot-key above, you would nuke the entire application, closing all the tabs and all seven PDFs. The hot-keys below allow you to close only the instance of the application you have in focus, whether that's a single tab or a particular PDF.

Windows: Hold Ctrl while you press w.

Mac: Hold Cmd while you press w.

## Switch Between Applications

Windows: Hold Alt while pressing Tab successively until the focus is on the application you wish to switch to.

Mac: Hold Cmd while pressing Tab successively until the focus is on the application you wish to switch to.

## Switch Within an Application

This hot-key allows you to move between instances within a single application. For example, if you have 10 tabs open and you need to focus on a different tab, you can easily switch which tab you are focused on.

Windows: Hold Ctrl while pressing Tab successively until the focus is on the part of the application you wish to switch to.

Mac: Hold Ctrl while pressing Tab successively until the focus is on the part of the application you wish to switch to.

## Search

Windows: Hold Ctrl while pressing f, then type the search term.

Mac: Hold Cmd while pressing f, then type the search term.

## BROWSER HOT-KEYS

This set of hot-keys works while using Chrome, the most popular browser. These hot-keys will probably work on other browsers as well. All the major browsers have the functionality described below.

## New Tab

Windows: Hold Ctrl while pressing t.

Mac: Hold Cmd while pressing t.

## Select URL

Windows: Hold Ctrl while pressing l.

Mac: Hold Cmd while pressing l.

## Zoom

Windows: Hold Ctrl while pressing + (zooms in), - (zooms out), or 0 (resets the zoom).

Mac: Hold Cmd while pressing + (zooms in), - (zooms out), or 0 (resets the zoom).

## Restore Previously Closed Tab(s)

This is super handy when you accidentally close a tab you don't remember how to get to. This hot-key keeps you from having to dig around in your browser history, hoping you can locate the lost tab. Pro tip: if the entire browser is accidentally closed, open the browser and then use this hot-key to reopen all of the previously closed tabs at one time.

Windows: Hold Ctrl and Shift while pressing t.

Mac: Hold Cmd and Shift while pressing t.

## Vimium

*Figure 26  Vimium allows me to navigate sites using only the keyboard.*

chrome.google.com/webstore/detail/vimium/dbepggeogbaib
hgnhhndojpepiihcmeb

This Chrome extension is not technically a hot-key, but I've
included it here because it creates a universal hot-key on any
page you browse to. All you have to do is hit the f key, and letters
appear over each of the links on the page. Then you type the
letter or letters above the link you'd like to "click," and your
browser follows the link, without ever involving your mouse.

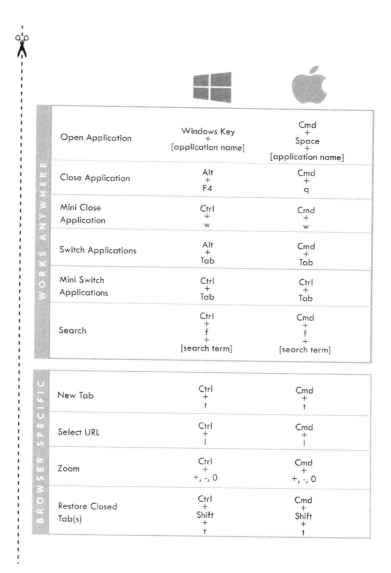

| | Windows | Apple |
|---|---|---|
| **WORKS ANYWHERE** | | |
| Open Application | Windows Key + [application name] | Cmd + Space + [application name] |
| Close Application | Alt + F4 | Cmd + q |
| Mini Close Application | Ctrl + w | Cmd + w |
| Switch Applications | Alt + Tab | Cmd + Tab |
| Mini Switch Applications | Ctrl + Tab | Ctrl + Tab |
| Search | Ctrl + f + [search term] | Cmd + f + [search term] |
| **BROWSER SPECIFIC** | | |
| New Tab | Ctrl + t | Cmd + t |
| Select URL | Ctrl + l | Cmd + l |
| Zoom | Ctrl + +, -, 0 | Cmd + +, -, 0 |
| Restore Closed Tab(s) | Ctrl + Shift + t | Cmd + Shift + t |

*Figure 27  Hot-Key Cheat Sheet.*

At this point, you are well equipped and you know the tricks, but understanding a kick-flip and being able to do a kick-flip are two entirely different things. I've included a script below that will allow you to try out your new skills. The first time or two, go ahead and peek at your cheat sheet when you need to. Then, see if you can make it through the script without referring to the cheat sheet.

Once you are feeling confident, try making your way through the script with your trackpad disabled. On Windows machines, you can often double tap the upper left-hand corner of the trackpad to disable it temporarily. If you are using a Mac, you can configure your trackpad to turn off by checking "Ignore Built-in Trackpad" in the accessibility settings and plugging in an external trackpad that you hide from yourself. Think of yourself as Hernán Cortés, who famously sunk his ships during the Spanish Conquest to keep his troops from turning on him.

## Practice Script

Open browser

Close browser

Open browser

Go to google.com

Search "mongol rally"

Open a new tab

Search from URL for "population of Mongolia"

Switch back to first tab

Remove first tab

Open a new tab

Search from URL for "happiest country in the world"

Close browser

Open browser

Go to wikipedia.com

On that tab, replace the URL with google.com

Open another tab for yahoo.com

Open another tab for craigslist.com

Close the tab for yahoo

Reopen the yahoo tab

Close the browser

Open browser

Reopen all three tabs

Zoom in to craigslist

Zoom out of craigslist until you can't read the font

Reset the zoom on craigslist

Search the craigslist landing page to for the word "creative"

Close the craigslist tab

Navigate to the yahoo tab

Search for "style"

Replace the yahoo tab URL with ebay.com

Close the browser

Congratulations! You made it through the hot-key gauntlet. Come back to this script a few times over the next couple of weeks and test yourself to make sure you haven't forgotten any of these hot-keys. Be prepared to blow the minds of your friends and family when you share one or two of these with them. I claim no responsibility if they begin asking you to fix their broken computers.

# SET YOUR GOALS

The time has come to set a goal related to becoming the power user you were meant to be. Set at least one goal for the way you'll implement what you've learned in this chapter over the next week.

**If I do not meet my goal, I will give $_____ to _____.**

**My goal:**

Can't choose a single goal to focus on? Pick two or three! If you are looking for suggestions, here's a list to get you thinking:

- Use a clipboard manager.

- Use a windows manager.

- Turn Caps Lock into a Ctrl key.

- Use hot-keys to open and close your applications.

- Use hot-keys to manage tabs in your browser.

This chapter is fifth for a reason: It is not easy. At this point, we are pushing on some pretty deep-seated ideas about how your devices work and are replacing old habits with Vin Diesel ones. In the next chapter, we'll look at a couple of places where you can almost certainly free up some time in your schedule: television and gaming. We'll also explore your interests in the real world, whether that involves career aspirations or tinkering in your garage.

# SIX

## RECLAIM: Purposeful Leisure

*The more you try to do, the less you actually accomplish... execution should be aimed at a small number of wildly important goals.*

CAL NEWPORT

In this chapter, we'll talk about our relationship to work and personal time. By presenting evidence on the effects of excessive television use and videogaming, I'll set the stage for a deeper investigation of our career and personal aspirations. By the close of the chapter, you should have a good sense of where you want to go and have a better idea of how to get there.

Over the last few decades, work as we know it has changed considerably. Arguably the best and worst thing brought about by the internet has been the fact that today many folks can work from anywhere. The result has been a reduction in the traditional structure of our work lives, fewer boundaries around when we are and when we are not working. According to the U.S. Travel Association, Americans are taking the lowest levels of vacation time in 40 years[64]. Sixty-one percent of us are working at some point during the vacation we do take[65]. Slate claims that 30% of us work on weekends[66], while 60% of us work outside of traditional work hours, with one in five of us responding to after-hours emails as if we were on the clock[67]. Lunch has been all but killed by the rush to get all of our work done. Only one in three of us leaves our desk for lunch[68], and the average lunch "hour" has shrunk to less than 30 minutes[69]. Meanwhile, self-reported stress levels have risen 10-30% in the past three decades[70]. The CDC quoted the Towers Watson Survey in warning that stress was the number one workforce health issue[71].

There is more to the story than simply overworked employees, however. Workers are increasingly slacking off during work. The average American worker is now spending more than eight hours per work week on the job but off task. More than half of this corporate slacking takes place on a mobile device[72]. Studies carried out by the Universities of Wurzburg & Nottingham Trent found that when workers didn't have access to their smartphones, they became 26% more productive[73].

[64] Cooper, "Why Rest Is so Important (and Why You're Not Getting Enough)."
[65] "Average U.S. Employee Only Takes Half of Earned Vacation Time; Glassdoor Employment Confidence Survey (Q1 2014)."
[66] Weissmann, "Americans, Ever Hateful of Leisure, Are More Likely to Work Nights and Weekends."
[67] Brooks, May 17, and EST, "Checking Email After Work Won't Make You Miserable."
[68] Luckerson, "Is Lunch a Waste of Time — or a Productivity Booster?"
[69] Hills, "Whatever Happened to the Lunch Hour?"
[70] Neal, "Stress Levels Soar in America by up to 30% in 30 Years."
[71] Ganster et al., "Intervening for Work Stress."
[72] "WORKING HARD OR HARDLY WORKING?"
[73] "Kaspersky Lab Study Proves Smartphones Distract Workers and

To work harder during work and to disengage from work at times when you are not on the clock:

## Don't work near your mobile device.

There is plenty of evidence that our personal devices take up some of our mental real estate, diminishing our cognitive ability[74] and experiences of closeness and trust[75]. While you are working, keep your smartphone stowed away or turned off to give work your full attention.

## Eat lunch with other people.

Evidence of the benefits of socializing with coworkers has been mounting for decades[76]. Loneliness was recently found to be a stronger predictor of premature death than obesity or smoking 15 cigarettes a day[77]. Aside from warding off loneliness, eating with others builds social capital and good will that can be drawn upon when difficult situations arise in the workplace.

## Take vacation without your devices.

Data collected by the Institute for Work and Families tells us that less than half of us take all of our vacation days. There seems to be a worry that if we take too much vacation, we'll be labeled as slackers or that coworkers will realize they can do without us. Fortunately for vacationers, there is little evidence that taking vacations affects future promotions or raises[78].

---

Decrease Productivity."
[74] Ward et al., "Brain Drain."
[75] Carr, "How Smartphones Hijack Our Minds."
[76] Robinson and Pentland, "Workplace Socializing Is Productive."
[77] Latson, "A Cure for Disconnection."
[78] "The Research."

Meanwhile, vacation does reduce the risk of heart disease and increases lifespan[79]. Another worry is that while we're on vacation, coworkers will need us to take care of some specialized task only we know how to do. There is no easy way to say this, so I'll just say it: We aren't as important as we think we are. The work world will keep turning without you or me for a few days. If you are still sure things will go south without your involvement, consider Tim Ferriss' advice: "Develop the habit of letting small bad things happen. If you don't, you'll never find time for the life-changing big things"[80].

Now that we've discussed ways to manage our relationship with work, television and gaming will take center stage in the next section as we consider the super-sized place they take in our free time.

## TELEVISION

Depending on which source you believe, Americans spend 1.4[81] to 2.5[82] months of every year sitting in front of the boob tube. The downside is that we've known for decades about the health risks associated with watching television. Many studies have connected television to obesity. Possibly the most damning study demonstrated that television habits as a child predict obesity in adulthood[83]. Television even increases risk of death[84]. An expert from the Mayo Clinic went so far as to describe the

---

[79] Cooper, "Why Rest Is so Important (and Why You're Not Getting Enough)."

[80] Newport, *Deep Work*.

[81] "American Time Use Survey."

[82] Rosen, "Watching TV Leads to Obesity."

[83] "Television Watching and 'Sit Time.'"

[84] Gardner, "TV Watching Raises Risk of Health Problems, Dying Young."

risks of watching television as "similar to what you see with high cholesterol or blood pressure or smoking"[85]. This description is not too surprising, given the association between television and obesity, paired with obesity's connection to type II diabetes, heart disease, and high blood pressure[86]. In fact, just watching a character in a television program experiencing stress can cause a release of the stress hormone, cortisol, in viewers[87]. Other well-documented side effects of television viewing include violent behavior, less time spent reading, physical inactivity, and negative impact on sleep[88].

Compared to the total amount of time we spend reading—less than five days per year[89]—we get a pretty clear picture of just how much more we enjoy television, despite the many benefits of reading. An activity that is intellectual in nature (like reading) slows the rate of mental decline as aging occurs[90]. Reading lowers stress levels 67% more than listening to music or playing video games[91]. Finally, increased reading results in a longer life; one study found that, on average, people who read books live almost two years longer than non-book readers[92].

Despite the rise of the internet and smartphones, we've been watching as much television as ever[93], and the shows seem to be getting better. Netflix released a study that demonstrated just how addictive new series have become. For some of the most

---

[85] Gardner.
[86] "Overweight & Obesity Statistics | NIDDK."
[87] Perry, "Stress Can Be Transmitted through TV Screen."
[88] Rosen, "Watching TV Leads to Obesity."
[89] Stephen, "You Won't Believe How Little Americans Read."
[90] Specktor, "Here's Why Your Brain Needs You to Read Every Day."
[91] Specktor.
[92] Flood, "Book up for a Longer Life."
[93] Carr, *Utopia Is Creepy.*

popular shows (*Breaking Bad, Scandal,* and *The Walking Dead*), it took just two episodes to get viewers so hooked that 70% of them continued watching to the end of the season[94]. Comparing today's shows to older television series—like *Family Matters, Friends,* or *Seinfeld*—you'll find that older shows were driven by familiar characters placed in varied situations, whereas the bulk of today's television is more like one big movie with episodic cliffhanger endings throughout.

If your response to the paragraphs above was a resigned sigh or shoulder shrug, I get it. Television can be a relaxing way to end a hard day. At least take a minute to figure out just how much time you are spending watching it—which is now easy to do, thanks to a site called Tiii.me (tiii.me). You just type in which shows and how many seasons you've watched, and the site totals the time you spent watching each show, as well as an overall total of all your shows. If you need to jog your memory of what you've been watching, try these links to your viewing histories on popular streaming platforms:

netflix.com/ViewingActivity

amazon.com/gp/yourstore/iyr/ref=pd_ys_iyr_edit_watched?ie=UTF8&collection=watched

secure.hulu.com/account/history

If you haven't already, turn off the autoplay feature on all of your streaming services. When autoplay is on (which is often the default setting), the next episode of whatever show you're watching will start automatically. I believe users should be in control of their own viewing habits. Don't let the technology

---

[94] Alter, *Irresistible.*

decide for you.

## GAMING

When I was growing up, my family had a strict rule against owning a gaming console. That said, once we got a computer, we began playing DigDug and Minesweeper. That was all child's play—literally and figuratively—until my brother got a game called Command & Conquer. The game was so fun that on more than one night as I fell asleep, I'd hear one of the characters, Tanya, shout, "Let's rock!" before detonating an enemy building. If I snuck downstairs, I would find none other than my dad, up late playing my brother's game.

In the next two paragraphs, I'll break down some confusing gaming research about the impact that video games are having on gamers. Keep in mind that one of the challenges with video game research is that it is difficult to make generalizations, given how many and how varied games there are.

Is there any evidence that games can be a force for good? Some prosocial games—games that encourage players to act out positive social behaviors—have been shown to "positively influence young people's emotional state, self-esteem, optimism, vitality, resilience, engagement, relationships, sense of competence, self-acceptance, and social connections and functioning." Research on casual games—the kind you can buy at the mall—showed that stress, anxiety, and depression could be reduced by play[95]. There are also lots of educational games that can shorten time it takes learners to get feedback after applying new knowledge.

---

[95] Calvo and Peters, *Positive Computing*.

However, there is a dark side to gaming, particularly to heavy gaming. Not all games are created equal, and many games expose our minds to violence and aggression that can be unhealthy. According to the authors of *Positive Computing*, "exposure to violent video games has consistently been shown to increase aggression, desensitize to violence, and reduce prosocial behavior"[96]. There is also a link between heavy video game use and attention deficit and hyperactivity measures[97]. This could be because competition between gaming firms has forced developers to make the games more and more stimulating. If players spend large amounts of time in a hyper-stimulated state, the real world starts to feel... well... boring. In the education context, overuse of quick feedback cycles, where the answer is always one small step beyond what you learned previously, could lead learners to give up quickly when faced with unfamiliar or complex problems, which don't yield quick results.

## Who Are Gamers?

"Historically most gamers have been men, but the gaming world has begun to appeal to women and other underserved groups. In fact, in August 2014, women over the age of 18 became the largest demographic in gaming. They represent 36% of gamers, whereas men over the age of 18 make up 35% of all gamers"[98]. This change has been helped along by browser and smartphone gaming. Farmville, for a time Facebook's most popular game, was so popular that one in 10 Americans had played[99]. Sixty-seven percent of smartphone users have gaming apps

---

[96] Calvo and Peters.
[97] Carr, *Utopia Is Creepy.*
[98] Alter, *Irresistible.*
[99] Alter.

installed[100]. A survey of eighth graders and high school seniors found that both groups spend about an hour and a half gaming each day[101]. That stat can be somewhat misleading, though. While 27% of teens play for less than an hour per week, 9% play for more than 40 hours per week[102].

If you are gaming for more than 40 hours a week, chances are high there has been some relationship blow-back. It's also likely that you are playing a highly addictive game. The most addictive games have three main elements that make them hard to stop playing: immersion in the game, regular achievements, and social connections mediated by the game[103].

## A PATH FORWARD

We know that gaming can be unhealthy, but it isn't all bad. How do you make informed choices amid so much contradictory messaging? For one, decide how much time you want to spend gaming, and don't go over. If you're spending over 40 hours a week gaming, try to think rationally about that. Forty hours a week of anything will have massive implications for those around you. Certainly, if I wanted to paint or golf or bowl for 40 hours a week, my family would have a conversation about it first—why should gaming be any different? The other concern I have about gaming involves the activities that gaming displaces. If gaming causes you to miss out on regular in-person moments with loved ones, your life will suffer, regardless of the quality of the game. Below are a few tips I recommend for people struggling to find a healthy balance with games.

---

[100] "Mobile Metrix."
[101] Twenge, *IGen.*
[102] Twenge.
[103] Alter, *Irresistible.*

## Schedule Your Gaming

Since console games have become networked, more and more often there are other people in cyberspace depending on us to play with them. Combine this with family members who grew up in an era when games were able to be paused, and you have a recipe for conflict. By discussing and scheduling sessions beforehand, family members can lay their expectations out in the open and avoid some frustration. Another idea is to limit your sessions by putting your console on an outlet timer. If you use a smartphone app, try the methods listed in Chapter 3 to control your use. AppDetox (Android) and Restrictions (iOS) are great ways to keep yourself from unintentionally wasting time with low-quality games.

## Choose Games Wisely

If a game is immersive, achievement-oriented, and contains a social element, it will likely be addictive. Find games that are missing at least one of these elements to keep yourself from losing your agency as you play.

...

Television and gaming can take up an enormous amount of time. They also can leave you feeling stressed and hyper-aroused, which makes them a questionable choice when needing to unwind. If you are having a very hard time moderating your use, please reach out to a professional psychologist or psychiatrist.

Finally, television and gaming both take place across large chunks of continuous time. It is easy to excuse spending hours a day on our phones because we rationalize that the phone time fills in the margins of our lives, the boring bits we just want to get through. Television and gaming are the opposite. If you are like most Americans, cutting down or eliminating these two will open up huge swaths of time in your schedule. Use that time to connect with those around you and to pursue the passions we'll investigate in the next section.

## PASSION MAPPING

The following process was originally invented by my wife. I was a couple of years out of grad school, struggling to find my direction. She unknowingly invented a process we've since repeated many times when seeking clarity and resolve despite living in a world full of uncertainty and doubt.

I've included two separate versions of the passion map. The first focuses on professional aspirations. The second will help you figure out what pursuits are most worthy of your limited personal time.

**Follow the instructions below to create your passion maps:**

First, you'll work on your professional passion map.

In the upper left corner of the upcoming blank page, write your top four skills in ascending order, culminating in what you consider to be your most valuable skill.

Write your name in the center.

Surround your name with four to six career options.

Under each career option, write two adjectives that describe someone who does this activity well.

Rate each career option in terms of income from $ to $$$.

Rate each career option in terms of happiness from :( to :| to :).

Rate each career option's benefits (e.g., health insurance, vacation time) from B to BBB.

Rate how much each career option involves technology from 000000 to 010101 to 111111.

Rate each career option's required time commitment from one clock to three clocks.

Add a stress emoji to each career option that is stressful.

Add a peace sign to each career option that makes the world a better place.

Add a butterfly to any career options that are social.

Add zzz's to any career options that are delayable.

Add a stick family to any career options that can be pursued while maintaining healthy work/life balance.

Add a Pro for pursuing each career option.

Add a Con to pursuing each career option.

Add an upward arrow for any career option that involves quick advancement.

For each career option, add the number of your skills that apply to the career option. Circle each number.

Now, cross out two to four of the career options.

Add stars to the remaining career options until they are ranked from most stars to least.

List two things you do for each remaining career option that are productive and two that feel productive but upon close examination are not.

# Professional Passion Map

Next, create your hobby passion map.

In the upper left corner of the upcoming blank page, write your top four skills in ascending order, culminating in what you consider to be your most valuable skill.

Write your name in the center.

Surround your name with four to six hobbies.

Under each hobby, write two adjectives that describe someone who does this activity well.

Rate each hobby in terms of cost from $ to $$$.

Rate each hobby in terms of happiness from :( to :| to :).

Rate each hobby's benefits (e.g., side money, fulfillment, usefulness in your home) from B to BBB.

Rate how much each hobby involves technology from 000000 to 010101 to 111111.

Rate each hobby's required time commitment from one clock to three clocks.

Add a stress emoji to each hobby that is stressful.

Add a peace sign to any hobbies that make the world a better place.

Add a butterfly to any hobbies that are social.

Add zzz's to any hobbies that are delayable.

Add a stick family to any hobbies that can be pursued while maintaining healthy work/life balance.

Add a Pro for pursuing each hobby.

Add a Con to pursuing each hobby.

Add an upward arrow for any hobby that involves quick advancement.

For each hobby, add the number of your skills that apply to the hobby. Circle each number.

Now, cross out two to four of the hobbies.

Add stars to the remaining hobbies until they are ranked from most stars to least.

List two things you do for each remaining hobby that are productive and two that feel productive but upon close examination are not.

A Guide to Mindful Technology Use

# Hobby Passion Map

Your passion maps are looking good. By forcing yourself to look at your passions through various lenses, you've narrowed down your pursuits to a few of what Cal Newport calls your "small number of wildly important goals"[104]. You are ready to conquer the world. This might sound like a buzzkill, but get out your calendar. Give it a hard look. Do you have time to pursue your interests? What will have to be sacrificed in order to succeed? Plan time to pursue these interests. Set aside blocks of time when you will invest in your career and hobby.

One of the casualties of our always-connected lives is that we do less advance planning. After all, why bother deciding when and where to meet up when I can just call or text when I'm in the area? Greater flexibility would seem to beget greater happiness. Unfortunately, a large component of happiness is anticipation of good things[105]. So, if you don't plan ahead, you miss out on a good portion of happiness. For example, think of a vacation to Mexico. If you book your flight three or four months in advance, you'll spend time before your trip thinking about how much fun your trip will be. Which type of margarita will we get first? Should we scuba dive? Are there black sand beaches in Mexico? Those thoughts give you little nuggets of happiness that can help you through the low points that occur between booking the flight and taking the trip.

---

104 Newport, *Deep Work*.
105 Rubin, "Get More Bang for Your Happiness Buck."

# SET YOUR GOALS

As we close the chapter, I encourage you to set two goals. The first goal should specify a way you'll divest some of your time away from an activity (e.g., less television or gaming). Then, set a time investment goal. Whether you plan to cook dinner from scratch, play board games, reach out to old friends, join a sports league, brew your own beer, collect rare coins, get on the treadmill, write a book, read a novel, install shelves, volunteer—the possibilities are endless. The world is still full of interesting activities you can explore.

**If I do not meet my goals, I will give $_____ to _____.**

**My time *reclaiming* goal:**

Can't think of a way to reclaim part of your day? Consider:

- Limit television to one episode per day.

- Limit gaming to the weekend.

- Turn off autoplay on YouTube, Netflix, and Hulu.

**My time *investment* goal:**

It is a difficult and unending process, trying to get the way you spend your time to match up with your values. With some commitment, patience, and practice, I hope you are able to point yourself in a healthy, fulfilling direction and paddle toward it. If you fail, don't be discouraged—keep reconfiguring and rearranging your environment to set yourself up for another chance.

In the next chapter, we'll explore the ways corporations and governments are seeking access to your digital footprint. I'll give context for the security-privacy debates and practical suggestions if you are seeking ways to avoid prying eyes.

# SEVEN

## PROTECT: Reducing Your Digital Footprint

*Knowledge has become transparent. We look out the window of the internet even as the internet looks back in.*

MICHAEL P. LYNCH

Several years ago, while living in Ecuador, I found myself at the base camp of a massive volcano called Cotopaxi. I'd been on top of a few "fourteeners" (peaks over 14,000 feet tall) but never to heights within shouting distance of Cotopaxi. Over dinner, one of the other climbers on our team, a Canadian, tried to convince us of one of the most ridiculous conspiracies I'd ever heard. He claimed that the U.S. government was snooping on everyone's internet traffic. He cited circumstantial evidence, massive data storage facilities in deserts, and a spike in the price of computer memory, all due to the government effectively swallowing the global supply. He'd rigged up a cockamamie system for getting confidential messages back to his family. Bit torrents, cron jobs, encryption, and other gobbledygook were required to keep from being watched and heard. I argued back with the usual arguments I use against conspiracy theorists: a) this is unlikely and b) even if it were true, who cares? That night I tossed and turned in my sleeping bag. Four months later, Edward Snowden, a government contractor turned whistleblower, provided concrete evidence for everything this paranoid Canadian had most feared.

This chapter will cover a lot of ground. It will help you understand the history and driving factors that have brought us to today's debate over security and privacy. I'll attempt to give you a balanced perspective, starting with some important moments in the history of the internet.

In case you aren't old enough to remember the beginnings of the internet, it was terrible. You had to use a CD-ROM to add time to your AOL account. Most websites were ugly, homemade, and inaccurate enough that librarians would warn against relying too heavily on sources found online. People would tell each other about individual websites. "Have you heard about Ask Jeeves?" You may have had an email account, but the internet wasn't safe, and your address was probably something like soccerdude16@aol.com.

It is important to remember, though, that it is only in retrospect that those early days seem sluggish, disorganized, a wild west of sorts. You were happy as a clam that you could type a URL and get something intelligible to show up. If you were really savvy, maybe you created your own page through Geocities or AngelFire, among the first website builders that didn't require coding skills. This straightforward exchange of URL-for-website summarizes what we today refer to as Web 1.0. Most of the pages lacked any meaningful interaction. They were essentially personalized billboards.

Fortunately, Web 2.0 rescued us with its heavier use of JavaScript for interaction. Some sites began requiring us to create accounts and then to log in and out before and after each visit. That allowed them to keep track of us a little bit better and allowed us to interact with other people online in less anonymous ways. MySpace and Facebook were on the cutting edge of this trend. We dropped DogPile, AltaVista, and Yahoo for Google. MySpace became a backwater for local bands, while masses of college students flocked to the initially-exclusive Facebook. Nearly every ecommerce site was left in Amazon's dust.

A similar trend took place in the phone market. While cell phones were initially dominated by brands like Nokia and Motorola, in 2007 Steve Jobs introduced the iPhone. The era of the smartphone was born. Blackberries, iPhones, and early Android phones transformed the way we connect to the internet. Communications companies struggled to beef up infrastructure, hoping they could handle the tsunami of mobile data. After a few years, apps—small applications designed for smartphones—became the next innovative space for companies hoping to reach customers with everything from coupons to radical news to the assets of strangers (e.g., Uber, Lyft, Airbnb).

The cloud became increasingly important and talked about, even if not completely understood by the average consumer. The cloud was developed to support all of the wildly fluctuating traffic that supported users and their browsers and smartphones. Traditionally, companies managed and ran their own web servers—computers that ship information out to customer devices upon request. The cloud represents the same capabilities being outsourced to a company that specializes in supporting the internet's more mundane functions. For a few lucky unicorns, companies like Netflix, Slack, and Reddit, viral success created previously unimagined traffic that is handled mostly gracefully by cloud providers. With that much data, we needed a new name to describe the phenomenon: "big data."

One of the rarely discussed, decidedly unsexy changes that took place in the late aughts and into the '10s was hiding in plain sight. In 2014, in an address to a Congressional subcommittee, Dr. Craig Labovitz spelled out what so many had overlooked: Control over the internet had drastically changed. As he explained, at one point thousands of companies meaningfully contributed to internet traffic, but that wasn't—and isn't—the case anymore. Dr. Labovitz reported, "By 2009 half of all internet traffic originated in less than 150 large content and content-distribution companies." At the time of his 2014 testimony, "Just 30 companies, including Netflix and Google, contribute[d] on average more than one half of all internet traffic during prime-time hours"[106]. So why does all of this matter? In the next section, I'll explain the consequences of plummeting internet traffic diversity.

## SURVEILLANCE CAPITALISM

The main result of this consolidation has been in the analytics industry. Seventy-five percent of the top million web sites have Google Analytics installed, meaning Google will keep track of your site's traffic details in exchange for collating it with their own databases that store most of your page visits all over the web[107]. Other companies have to be more creative. The social media platforms use their social widgets—those little icons encouraging you to share whatever you are looking at with your network—to track you across the web[108]. Amazon, which already knows about your purchases, can tell from their Amazon

---

[106] "Comcast Time Warner Cable Merger Video."
[107] "Privacy Mythbusting #6."
[108] Acar et al., "Facebook Tracking Through Social Plug-Ins."

Web Services analytics which companies are experiencing explosive growth. Most of the major sites are sucking up all kinds of data about how you use their sites, via the items you hover on, click, or get distracted by. Some experts use the term "data exhaust" to suggest that like car exhaust, data is unintentionally created by people as they travel around on the web. However, most user behavior is collected by an army of engineers who carefully craft ways to pick up on users' intentions via anything browsers and app platforms will allow them to access.

To illustrate the extent of the data collection, consider the following excerpt from journalist Robert Scheer's book *They Know Everything About You: How Data-Collecting Corporations and Snooping Government Agencies Are Destroying Democracy.*

> When any reader initially visits nytimes.com, the site sets what are known as first-party cookies. These bits of unique text allow the domain visited to identify you, and to track your activity on the site—permitting, for example, the paper to determine which articles are the most popular with which readers.

> When you conduct a search of the site, information about that query is sent over to Google, which operates the search box at the top of the screen. After scrolling down the page, you might choose to play a video that appears in the middle of the home page. That video, hosted by YouTube, a Google-owned company, sets cookies on your browser that send your search and viewing history to its parent company, which then stores it indefinitely and combines it with your other data to compile a more complete picture of you.

Under that video and linked to each item of content on the site are social "widgets," the Facebook "like" button and the Google+ button invariably among them. You may elect not to use those tools to share any *Times* item with your social media network. No matter; so long as you've used the widget hosts' services, these hosts will collect your data anyway and correlate it with the data they've gathered from your visits to other sites featuring widgets, which may range from shopping to porn sites.

[...]

In addition, there is a plethora of advertisements that dot the edges of the site. The instant that you visit a page, advertisers bid in a real-time auction for the chance to appear on your screen. The ads employ a number of tracking mechanisms, many of which are difficult to block or delete. Those mechanisms, including third-party cookies—a unique string of characters used to identify users (sort of like a social security number) and set by a party that is not the web domain visited—are used to track your online activities when you leave the first-party site[109].

That passage gives you a good sense of just how sophisticated trackers have become. To get a firsthand experience of browser-based surveillance, visit the site ClickClickClickClick (clickclickclick.click). The site listens to the ways you interact with the page and comments on your actions, echoing data back to you that can be easily collected by any site. Because some folks got savvy and disabled cookies, companies found a way to eliminate the need for them by inventing a process called

---

[109] Scheer, *They Know Everything About You.*

"browser fingerprinting." For a demonstration, visit Nothing Private (nothingprivate.ml). By storing a unique ID based on browser details, companies know who you are, even in "incognito mode" with cookies disabled.

Recent news would suggest that our smartphones aren't private either. Facebook recently admitted to abusing permissions users granted during installation. The company "began uploading call and text logs from phones running Google's Android system in 2015"[110]. There are likely thousands of apps abusing the permissions granted by users. To understand how this might work, think about an app like Uber. The driver needs to know your location, so it makes perfect sense that the location permission is necessary for the app to work as intended. However, you were never guaranteed that Uber wouldn't continue collecting your location whenever it wanted. We know that Uber is now capable of collecting your location at any moment[111].

Another example of an abuse involves the microphone permission. A startup called Alphonso has embedded its software in more than 250 games in the Google Play and Apple app stores. Once you install the game and give it the microphone permission, it begins listening. It then analyzes the data that can reveal information, such as the television shows you watch, what movies you view, ads you've been exposed to, what you really think of Michelle...you get the idea[112]. While iOS devices have stricter permissions than Android[113], it is important to keep your

---

[110] Nakashima and Anderson, "How Facebook Was Able to Siphon off Phone Call and Text Logs."

[111] Conger, "Uber Begins Background Collection of Rider Location Data."

[112] Maheshwari, "That Game on Your Phone May Be Tracking What You're Watching on TV."

[113] "How to Live Without Google."

permissions up to date and to uninstall apps that you discover are abusing your trust.

You might be thinking, "I don't reveal much online" or "I'm not very active on social media." Unfortunately, the tech giants still know a lot about you. As Dr. Jennifer Golbeck, Director of the Human-Computer Interaction Lab at the University of Maryland, has pointed out, your likes reveal more about you than you realize. She noted that "liking" the curly fries Facebook page was an indication of a user's intelligence. What?!

Consider that the things we like are not always innate, rational, self-determined choices. We are a mixed bag of identities, whether those be cultural, familial, professional, religious, or otherwise. Within a given identity, we share preferences with others who are like us. In this way, ideas and preferences spread within groups, similar to the way a common cold might. So, something as silly as clicking "like" on curly fries communicates much more to an astute engineer than you may realize[114].

In essence, anything you reveal about yourself online gives away significant information about you, not because you have necessarily shared much information, but because of the largeness of the data set that your data is compared against. If you've only ever liked the curly fries page and have done nothing else, Facebook now knows you are, by proxy, intelligent. At this point, Facebook can look at all the other intelligent people who are revealing lots more personal data than you are and can begin to make sweeping—and disturbingly accurate—assumptions about you.

If you are freaking out at this point, take a few deep breaths.

---

[114] Golbeck, *Your Social Media "Likes" Expose More than You Think.*

Google CEO Eric Schmidt assures us it is all for our benefit—after all, "If you have something you don't want anyone to know, maybe you shouldn't be doing it in the first place"[115]. That is a pretty extreme view—at least outside of dystopian novels. So, why are companies collecting all this data?

There are two main reasons why companies are harvesting your data so aggressively. Recently, a third reason has begun to emerge as well.

## Targeted Advertising

This topic was discussed briefly in Chapter 3, but it bears repeating. Advertising was an information-starved industry prior to the tech giants. The best you could do was to advertise with a radio station that played music your target demographic liked. Or rent a billboard on the way to a place you knew your potential customer would be likely to frequent. Super Bowl commercials represent the pinnacle of this style of point-and-spray advertising. Then, along came Facebook and Google, promising to put your product in front of introverted Republicans who are likely to go to a bar in Manhattan on St. Patrick's Day. Or women between 25 and 34 who are single and not happy about it, living in Seattle's suburbs. Advertisers must have wept with gratitude.

## Captivating Content

As new players like Netflix and Hulu emerged and began creating television and movies, the industry titans of the silver screen began to look crotchety—less agile, less ready for the future. Increasingly, sophisticated analytics allow new producers

---

[115] Scheer, *They Know Everything About You.*

to create utterly addicting content. Even social media platforms are training their artificial intelligence algorithms to determine how good content is. Good is often based on interaction, not necessarily quality. Outrage, cute animals, anger, high-pitched pundits, lies, or national politics inflame the social media world—but when your main metric is time spent on the site, things appear to be going swimmingly.

## Dynamic Pricing

If you aren't familiar with this practice, brace yourself. Companies are using your data to price their products. Today the same product might cost three people three different amounts. If you've been scoping out prices for spring break flights, you could unknowingly be giving travel companies intel on just how desperate you are for a flight or hotel. Once they know you are planning a week in Cozumel, as the trip approaches they already know how much time you have left to book. A person in those shoes might be willing to pay a little more.

. . .

With so much data about us, new questions have begun to emerge about social media's obligations to society.

## Take a moment to answer the following questions.

Michael Shulson has suggested that social media companies, like Facebook, know who their alcoholics are[116]. Facebook currently has a team analyzing data to pick up on potential suicide attempts. After a team verifies the concern, they may

---

[116] Schulson, "If the Internet Is Addictive, Why Don't We Regulate It?"

alert authorities to intervene[117].

**Are these practices a boon for public health or an experimental trial being forced on society by a private corporation? What, if any, obligations do social media companies have when they discover health-related information?**

Michael Lynch writes in his book *The Internet of Us* that "once you are no longer recognized as a possible credible source of information—even about yourself—then the dominating class will excuse itself for ignoring your basic rights"[118]. As discussed in Chapter 3, even access to a limited number of "likes" can convey profound insights into your personality.

**Do you buy Michael Lynch's argument that big data's ability to predict our desires diminishes our individuality?**

Jonathan Taplin, a media studies professor, has criticized online platforms, saying, "YouTube claims it has no control over

---

[117] Isaac, "Facebook Offers Tools for Those Who Fear a Friend May Be Suicidal."

[118] Lynch, *The Internet of Us.*

what users post on its platform, but this is not true. You will notice that there is no porn on the platform. YouTube has very sophisticated content ID tools that screen for porn before it can ever be posted"[119]. The Fake News scandal in the wake of the 2016 election also cast doubt on arguments that platforms are not responsible for the content that users post.

**Do you consider platforms to have any responsibility for the legality or truthfulness of hosted content? Who, if anyone, should determine what is considered legal or true?**

## HELP IS HERE

You can fight back against corporate surveillance without losing most of the tech swag—free email, chat services, world-class search. Below is a list of my top recommendations.

### Opt Out of Targeted Advertising

Contrary to what Mark Zuckerberg believes, 68% of us oppose targeted advertising[120]. Following the links below won't stop anyone from collecting your data; it just asks them not to show you ads that are based on the data they collect from you.

bluekai.com/registry/

---

[119] Taplin, *Move Fast and Break Things.*
[120] Purcell, Brenner, and Rainie, "Search Engine Use 2012."

isapps.acxiom.com/optout/optout.aspx

networkadvertising.org/choices/

adssettings.google.com/authenticated

facebook.com/settings?tab=ads

## Ublock Origin

*Figure 28 Notice the huge ad in line with normal content.*

*Figure 29 Ad zapped!*

chrome.google.com/webstore/detail/ublock-origin/cjpalhdlnbpafiamejdnhcphjbkeiagm

Ublock Origin removes advertisements from your browsing experience. No more video ads, image ads, or text ads. Nearly every ad on the internet, targeted or otherwise, disappears after the one-click install of this tool.

## DuckDuckGo

*Figure 30  A look and feel similar to Google without the filter bubble.*

chrome.google.com/webstore/detail/duckduckgo-privacy-essent/bkdgflcldnnnapblkhphbgpggdiikppg

In 2009, Google began using 57 factors to personalize your search, anything from your location to your past searching behavior[121]. This prompted warnings of filter bubbles, echo chambers of the web where we would hear only the opinions and ideas we wanted to hear. Those hoping for a more universal, less personalized search option got together to build DuckDuckGo, a search engine that promises never to store information about its users.

An extra cool goodie bag comes with DuckDuckGo in the form

---

[121] Pariser, *The Filter Bubble.*

of "bangs." This feature allows you to quickly search on particular websites. For example, typing "!e nissan sentra 1998 tail light" will automatically transport you to eBay's results for your search. !a searches Amazon. !m searches your map provider of choice.

## Terms of Service; Didn't Read

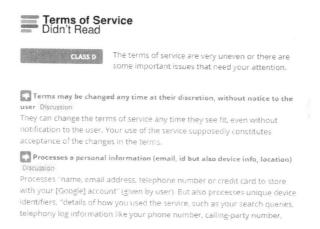

*Figure 31  Clicking on the icon gives you a digestible assessment of the terms of service.*

chrome.google.com/webstore/detail/terms-of-service-didn%E2%80%99t-r/hjdoplcnndgiblooccencgcggcoihigg

As someone who doesn't read fine print—millions of people can't all be wrong, right?—I will never be the first to cast a stone at those of you who don't either. Terms of Service; Didn't Read to the rescue. This Chrome extension summarizes the fine print terms of service we all ignore. It gives popular sites scores on the way they slice up legal rights related to their services. Questions like "If I remove a YouTube video from my account, does YouTube really delete the video?"—once shrouded in miles of legalese—suddenly become answerable. ("No" is the answer to that one.)

## Privacy Badger

*Figure 32  Privacy Badger automatically turns off trackers.*

chrome.google.com/webstore/detail/privacy-badger/pkehgijcmpdhfbdbbnkijodmdjhbjlgp

Created by the Electronic Freedom Foundation, Privacy Badger attempts to automatically disrupt trackers as you browse. This allows you to visit sites without Google—or anyone else, for that matter—knowing about it. If you want to bring anonymity back to your adventures online, this is a great first step. Another great feature that comes with Privacy Badger is the ability to remove social widgets from sites you visit. You'll never have to look at another Pinterest or Instagram icon prodding you to share that recipe for the butternut squash soup you are making.

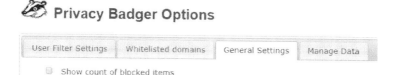

## Privacy Badger Options

| User Filter Settings | Whitelisted domains | General Settings | Manage Data |
| --- | --- | --- | --- |

☐ Show count of blocked items
☑ Replace social widgets

*Figure 33  For less clutter, check the "Replace social widgets" box in Privacy Badger's options.*

Apart from government intervention, corporations already had incentives to track users across the internet, noting not only which sites we spent time on—which we now realize are considerably less diverse than a decade ago—but also what we do while on those sites.

In the next section, we'll cover the mystery-shrouded security state that plucky Canadian tried to warn me about on a mountain in Ecuador.

### SECURITY STATE

In 2013, Edward Snowden, in partnership with *The Guardian* and *The Washington Post*, blew the lid off of the U.S. intelligence community's massive spying effort. Consider this statement by Snowden taken from *The Guardian* interview transcript:

> NSA [National Security Agency] and the intelligence community, in general, is [sic] focused on getting intelligence wherever it can, by any means possible, that it believes, on the grounds of sort of a self-certification, that they serve the national interest. Originally, we saw that focus very narrowly tailored as foreign intelligence gathered overseas. Now, increasingly, we see that it's happening domestically. And to do that, they—the

NSA—specifically targets the communications of everyone. It ingests them by default. It collects them in its system, and it filters them, and it analyzes them, and it measures them, and it stores them for periods of time, simply because that's the easiest, most efficient and most valuable way to achieve these ends[122].

What specifically do the Snowden documents reveal? They disclose that the U.S. intelligence community was involved in the following:

*Tapping into backbone internet cables*

*Accessing private corporate servers*

*Cracking and weakening encryption*

*Using spyware impervious to wiping a hard drive*

*Inspecting content of emails, chats, videos, voice messages, photos, social media*

*Monitoring call logs, YouTube video clicks, browsing history, phone geolocation*

These surveillance efforts were carried out with and without cooperation from corporations. When this came out, many were up in arms. How could this be legal!? Doesn't the Fourth Amendment protect Americans from warrantless searches? There are a couple of key legal maneuvers that have allowed the bulk collection of all of this data to take place. First, the Foreign Intelligence Surveillance Act created a secret court abbreviated as FISA. This court authorizes or denies requests made by

---

[122] "NSA Leaker Edward Snowden In His Own Words."

intelligence agencies hoping to get permission to investigate confidential matters. In the last 30 years, FISA has rejected only 11 of more than 30,000 such requests[123]. The other way intelligence agencies have circumvented constitutional restrictions has been by routing domestic information overseas. Telecoms like AT&T and Verizon agreed to route domestic communications to foreign locations where they could be inspected legally[124].

There is another side to this story. Encryption, while seemingly for our protection, has also allowed money laundering, drug purchasing, and child abuse image sharing to occur with impunity[125]. As tools available to criminals have grown increasingly sophisticated, law enforcement needs the ability and authority to pursue law and order in the networked world.

Unfortunately, our feelings of insecurity and our actual safety are not always calibrated correctly. My back-of-an-envelope calculation suggests that civilian Americans were more likely to be killed by a dog or cow than a terrorist between 2002 and 2013[126]. Many folks working for intelligence agencies would follow that stat with "you're welcome." This perspective is perhaps best expressed by Stewart Baker, who served in the NSA and Department of Homeland Security during the George W. Bush administration, when he said, "I'm always astonished how people are willing to abstract these decisions from the actual stakes. We're talking about trying to gather information

---

[123] Keller, *Democracy Betrayed.*
[124] Scheer, *They Know Everything About You.*
[125] Bartlett, *The Dark Net.*
[126] Ingraham, "Chart"; Jones and Bower, "American Deaths in Terrorism vs. Gun Violence in One Graph."

about people who are trying to kill us and who will succeed if we don't have robust information about their activities"[127].

## ENCRYPTION SALVATIONALISTS

Not everyone is satisfied with assurances from the intelligence community. For starters, the government has a gargantuan problem with the over-classification of documents[128]. Government officials promise they are foiling lots of terrorist plots but can't provide the public with details, because they're classified[129].

Protecting citizens from unwanted government surveillance has brought together a strange group from radical libertarians to mainstream liberals to the government itself. In the early days of the internet, a group known as cypherpunks, mainly libertarians, developed new ways to encrypt information—making it much more difficult for anyone who might want to decode a message to snoop. Their ethos is well-summarized by leader Chuck Hammill, who said, "For a fraction of the investment in time, money, and effort I might expend in trying to convince the state to abolish wiretapping and all forms of censorship...I can teach every libertarian who's interested how to use cryptography to abolish them unilaterally"[130]. These radical libertarians thought of the internet as a beautiful, organic experiment and wanted to make sure it remained open and free from state surveillance. This group of talented mathematicians and software engineers

---

[127] Timberg, "U.S. Threatened Massive Fine to Force Yahoo to Release Data."

[128] Goitein and Shapiro, "Reducing Overclassification Through Accountability."

[129] Sullivan, "NSA Head: Surveillance Helped Thwart More than 50 Terror Plots."

[130] Bartlett, *The Dark Net.*

would work hard to make encryption easily accessible to anyone who hoped to keep their messages secure.

As the Great Recession began in the twilight years of the George W. Bush presidency, the unity forged by 9/11 began to fall apart. Liberals began to criticize practices employed by the administration to obtain enemy intelligence. During his presidential campaign, Barack Obama called the Iraq War a mistake[131]. Thus, the issue of national security has remained a political issue, with Republicans willing to take more drastic measures to curb terrorism, whereas Democrats remain skeptical and want to ensure our government follows due process and doesn't persecute particular groups disproportionately. So, through a strange twist of fate, the left, in the arena of national security, has inherited the legacy of encryption and distrust of the government's assurances.

In an even stranger twist of events, the most commonly used encrypted browser, the Tor browser, was built by the government's U.S. Naval Research Laboratory and continues to be partially funded by the government[132].

...

Now that you have some political history on the movement to protect privacy, let's examine their core arguments. Many privacy advocates argue that privacy is a fundamental right. Citing the Fourth Amendment and other historical evidence, they believe privacy has intrinsic value. It has existed in every free society in some form and is important to preserve as technology continues to change our world. They would also cite

---

[131] "Obama Criticizes His Rivals on Iraq."
[132] Bartlett, The Dark Net.

statistics about the low number of civilian deaths from terrorism as evidence that the problem of terrorism simply isn't as large as officials would have us believe. Another argument against government surveillance points to historical moments in which hiding information from the government was, in fact, good. Invading Nazis during World War II provides a potent example. If Nazis had been able to see everyone's internet searches, wouldn't they have rounded up anyone who searched for "how to hide friends in your house"? The final argument that privacy advocates make is that the government, in particular the intelligence community, has a long history of overreach. In their view, when allowed to operate in the shadows with limited oversight, terrible things happen. Meddling with foreign countries' governments or threatening law-abiding Americans like Martin Luther King, Jr., the government has not always acted in accordance with our professed democratic values.

If you are swayed by the privacy advocates' arguments, below are a few tools to help you maintain your anonymity online and in real life.

## TOOLS FOR INCREASED ANONYMITY

### Have I Been Pwned?

haveibeenpwned.com

Pwned, pronounced p-owned, is internet slang for being deanonymized or outed. Have I Been Pwned? is a tool that allows you to find any instances when you may have been pwned, whether that be a part of a headline-grabbing breach like the Yahoo hack[133] or a smaller, less-publicized hack you never

---

[133] Roberts, "Yahoo Got Hacked Big Time."

found out about. Knowing which accounts may have had their passwords compromised will help you determine which of your other accounts may need a password change. It is worth emphasizing that this is the reason you should use different passwords for different accounts. After hackers get your email and password for one account, they visit other popular sites and see where else the combination will work.

### The Onion Router (Tor)

torproject.org

"In 2010, Tor was awarded the Free Software Foundation's Award for Projects of Social Benefit, in part for the service it provides for whistleblowers, human-rights campaigners, and activists in dissident movements"[134]. Tor is also the portal into the Dark Net, a world where anonymized Bitcoins can be spent on drugs and worse.

If only a tiny fraction of messages is fully encrypted, anyone hoping to snoop on a valuable message needs only grab fully encrypted messages and start hammering at them until they can crack in. If users create more fully encrypted messages, that makes the effort required to uncover any valuable message astronomically more difficult. Imagine spending days attempting to crack into a message only to find out that Larry in Reno, Nevada, just purchased a 12-pack of gray socks. Using Tor for regular browsing does provide cover traffic for those using the browser to protect human rights. Unfortunately, it also provides cover traffic for those using Tor to purchase or share child abuse images. As it is nearly impossible to weigh the costs versus benefits of using Tor, I can't fully recommend for or against

---

[134] Bartlett, *The Dark Net.*

using Tor.

## Faraday Cage

Although you need to be pretty kooky to own one of these, a faraday cage (or faraday pouch) provides extra security that you are not being tracked. If you are convinced, for example, that the government or someone else is using your own device to track you, surrounding your device with metal mesh disrupts any signals going to or from the device. Unfortunately, this also means your device won't connect to telecom towers. Think of it as airplane mode for those who don't believe airplane mode can stop the people tracking you. Even if you aren't that paranoid, a faraday cage can come in handy when you are overwhelmed and want some refuge from the onslaught of incoming messages and push notifications.

## Balance Required

In his book *A Guide for the Perplexed*, E. F. Schumacher argues that there are essentially two types of problems in the world, convergent and divergent ones[135]. Convergent problems are the easiest to solve because there is some essential form that most solutions bend toward. Think about the design of a bicycle or plane. Over time, the vast majority of them have begun to take a similar form. There may be three-wheeled bicycles and biplanes, but the vast majority of bicycles have two equal-sized wheels, and planes almost always have their engines mounted on the two wings located in the middle of the fuselage.

However, I've come to view the security versus privacy debate as a divergent problem. In this type of problem, if one of the

---

[135] Schumacher, *A Guide for the Perplexed*.

sides wins, society loses. If we are asked for perpetual support of our intelligence community without any interrogation of the results of their efforts, we risk living in an Orwellian dystopia where people disappear for crimes unnamed. On the other hand, if privacy advocates were to find a way to provide permanently secure encryption, crime carried out under the cloak of secrecy would carry on with impunity, and our law enforcement community would be unable to carry out the laws enacted by democratically elected officials. A divergent problem requires balance.

We need to know the current state of affairs and advocate for centrist policies. In the wake of 9/11 and the Snowden revelations, it is likely that we will need more pushback against government and corporate invasions of personal privacy before we are rebalanced. That said, the goal should be to have authorities we can trust and empower to carry out the difficult work required to keep citizens safe and free, all without compromising our collective values.

I hope this chapter has given you a new perspective or contextual framework for understanding future developments as our online world continues to evolve. We live in heady times where many political ideologies are scrambling to quiet centrist, compromise-friendly views. I sense the beginning of a change and hope for a future in which we stop demanding dogmatic purity from elected officials but instead reward those who can forge agreements and find pragmatic solutions to our increasingly complex political landscape.

# SET YOUR GOALS

Depending on where you fall on the ideological spectrum, you may or may not be interested in a less public digital footprint. The goal setting instructions below offer concrete steps to protect your data or at least to keep your data from being used in targeted advertising.

**If I do not meet my goal, I will give $\_\_\_\_ to _____.**

**My goal:**

Here are a few ideas:

- Make DuckDuckGo your default search engine.

- Opt out of targeted advertising.

- Block internet advertising with Ublock Origin.

- Install Privacy Badger to avoid being tracked.

- Understand terms and conditions legalese with Terms of Service; Didn't Read.

If you disagree with my presentation of any of the political forces discussed in this chapter, it is my hope that you'll continue reading. The next chapter will give you valuable insights on how to change the way you view the internet, literally. From your phone to your laptop, I'll give you lots of ideas about how to restyle your digital spaces. We'll take a deep dive into a unique Chrome extension called Stylebot. Stylebot will transform you into a web wizard, slicing and dicing sites to your liking.

# EIGHT

## RESTYLE: An Internet as Unique as You

*My mission in life is not merely to survive but to thrive, and to do so with some passion, some compassion, some humor, and some style.*

MAYA ANGELOU

In earlier chapters, I've tried to hammer home my recipe for long-term habit change:

**Be ruthless with your environment,**

**but be compassionate towards yourself.**

This chapter will provide you with new ideas for reconfiguring your environment in ways that promote digital peace. The tools and strategies presented will vary in difficulty. We'll start with simple ideas that are easy to implement or install. Toward the end of the chapter, we'll focus more on advanced topics. This will involve understanding some web fundamentals. Although not as user-friendly as earlier suggestions, if you master a tool like Stylebot, you'll begin to feel power over your technology like never before.

How can you get ruthless with your digital environment and actively restyle your experience? We'll start by addressing ways to reconfigure your smartphone. Then, we'll move on to new ideas for changing your laptop.

## ALTER YOUR PHONE

### Tools-Only Homescreen[136]

*Figure 34 A distraction-free homescreen.*

Reorganizing your apps so that only tool-oriented apps are located on your homescreen will go a long way toward

---

[136] Harris, "Distracted in 2016?"

protecting your focus. My homescreen only has a few apps (calendar, flashlight, phone, text message, clock, and camera). When I open my phone, none of those apps beg for my attention through well-designed icons or red badges. Okay, so I was once distracted by my flashlight—but generally speaking, tools don't draw you away from your intentions. After a recent event, I spoke with an IT professional who said she was unable to use her phone without being sucked into all the alerts and notifications. She was planning to buy an old-fashioned watch. She realized that what often started as a few seconds checking the time turned into an extended session of scrolling through alerts.

## Type to Launch Apps[137]

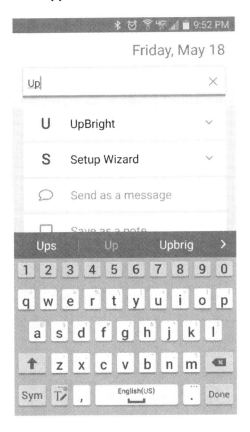

*Figure 35  Use Siempo to open an app by typing its name.*

Even if you move your distracting apps off of your homescreen, your thumb will memorize how to open them quickly. If you are on an iOS device, use the Spotlight feature, which is prebaked into the operating system, to type to launch apps. For Android users, adding a launcher is straightforward and interrupts the mindlessness of opening that same app again and again. I have

---

[137] Harris.

experimented with a few launchers and wholeheartedly recommend Siempo (getsiempo.com). Siempo includes a few other great features, such as replacing icons with uniform font, batching notifications on user-controlled intervals, randomizing the location of apps you flag as unproductive, and setting intentions.

## Human-Centric Notifications[138]

*Figure 36  Machine messages: No, thanks. Messages from humans: Yes, please.*

If you have more than a couple of apps installed, your phone is probably beeping, buzzing, pinging, and flashing for much of the day. Which apps' notifications are worth getting, and which can be safely turned off? A simple rule is to allow notifications that indicate another person reaching out to you. Silence the rest. If someone is trying to get in touch with you and has taken the time to send you a message, unless you are famous, that message

---

[138] Harris.

probably warrants some of your attention. It doesn't mean you need to respond immediately, but it is worth knowing about. On the other hand, if someone posts a photo you are in, or comments on a photo you are tagged in, or begins following you, machines are creating and sending you those notifications. You don't need those.

## Space by Dopamine Labs

*Figure 37  Create "spacified" shortcuts for your distracting apps.*

youjustneedspace.com

Space is a notable attempt to help people who want to limit the time they spend on certain apps but not quit using them entirely. Space takes you through a process by which you create new "spacified" shortcuts for each of your trouble apps. Then, it creates a pause between when you tap the icon and when the app loads to give you a moment to think through your decision, as if to say, "Is now really a good time to open Instagram?"

## No Infinite Scroll Apps

For most people, I firmly believe the only healthy place for certain types of apps is on a desktop or laptop computer, where addictive qualities can be more easily managed. The apps I consider too hard to use mindfully on your phone are any apps that contain an infinite scroll. These apps get you to jump on the thumb treadmill, swiping further and further down as new content pops into the frame. Designing an application that encourages users to look at it for extended periods is a telltale sign that your eyes and attention are being sold. Don't be a sucker—just remove these apps from your phone.

## Black and White Screen

In Android phones running versions 5.0 (Lollipop) and higher, if you enable developer mode, you can turn your phone's screen to black and white. To do so, search in the settings for developer options. Once you've turned the developer options on, search through the options until you find an option called "simulate color space." Choose "monochromacy."

If you are using an iOS device running version 8 or above, check out your accessibility settings in the vision section to activate grayscale.

Turning your device into black and white mode will significantly reduce the amount of stimulation you get from your phone. It also prevents one source of blue light in the evening, which has been shown to make it harder to fall asleep[139].

Up next, we'll investigate a few tweaks you can make to your laptop. Before you move on to the next section, take a few moments to work on your smartphone. The suggestions above will go a long way toward restoring sanity to your days, but they only work if you do them. Go ahead and try as many of the ideas as you can stomach. All of the changes I've suggested are undoable, should you later wish to switch things back to the way they were.

## ALTER YOUR LAPTOP

### Mercury Reader

*Figure 38  Read articles without distracting links leading you into the far corners of the web.*

chrome.google.com/webstore/detail/mercury-

---

[139] "Blue Light Has a Dark Side."

reader/oknpjjbmpnndlpmnhmekjpocelpnlfdi

If you read articles online, Mercury Reader is a godsend. This Chrome extension allows you to transform a page that contains an article into a distraction-free view by clicking on its rocket ship icon. Poof! All those alluring links along the side of the article, complete with click-bait photos, disappear and you are left in peace. You now have a fighting chance of making it to the end of the article. Even with Mercury Reader, it can be difficult to get to the bottom if there are links within the article, leading to other interesting pages or articles. When you encounter a link you are interested in, next time try this: hold down Ctrl (Windows) or Cmd (Mac) as you click the link. That will open the link in a new tab without changing the focus of the browser to that new tab. So, you can keep reading as you were, while being confident that you won't forget about that interesting rabbit hole that will be waiting for you later.

## Text Mode

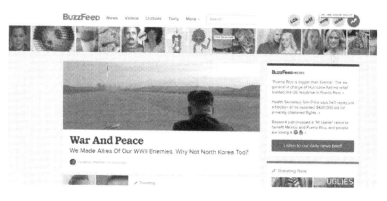

*Figure 39  Images all over the place, just begging to be clicked.*

*Figure 40  Text Mode tames the chaos by removing images.*

https://chrome.google.com/webstore/detail/text-mode/adelhekhakakocomdfejiipdnaadiiib

Images are powerful. Much of our browsing gets derailed by beautiful images pulling us from page to page. Text Mode, a Chrome extension, solves this issue by removing all images from the sites you visit. It also changes font to grayscale, which makes the web look a lot like a newspaper. Take that, BuzzFeed! Turn Text Mode on or off by clicking its icon.

## Black and White Screen

If you're keen to change your laptop into black and white mode, it couldn't be easier. On a Windows device, navigate to "Color Filter settings." Then switch on the "Turn on color filters" option and choose "Grayscale" from the options below. On a Mac, inside your "System Preferences," select "Universal Access." Inside the "Seeing" tab, check the "Use Grayscale" checkbox[140]. As with your smartphone, operating in grayscale

---

[140] Babauta, "A Practice For When You Find Yourself Annoyed by Other People."

limits the visual stimulation you experience on your laptop.

## THE INTERNET IN 10 MINUTES

If you are ready for more in-depth understanding of how the internet (and specifically your browser) works, here it comes. Some of what is discussed below applies to smartphone apps, but the main focus is on understanding how sites in a browser function so that we can change them with Stylebot later.

The first concept to grasp is the server-client relationship. Already confused? The client is you and your browser. The server is a computer somewhere that hands out pages to all the many clients. You can think of using the internet as going to a restaurant. When you've selected what you'd like (the site you want to look at), your waiter goes back and gets the kitchen to prepare it (this is the computer server's role) and brings it back to you (via your browser).

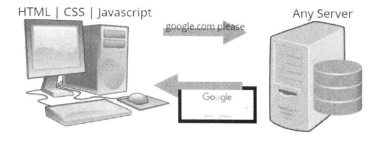

*Figure 41 You, the client, make requests to servers, which send back the page you've requested.*

It can get more complicated, but at a basic level, all sites follow that same request-response form. And just like at a restaurant, things are crazy in the kitchen (server). We really don't care what happens back there as long as our meal comes out looking and tasting good. In the same way, there are a number of computer languages and frameworks that servers use to prepare sites before sending them out. None of that matters as long as they can get something out the door that is palatable for you. So, what are you (the client) willing to accept?

## THREE PROGRAMMING LANGUAGES

It takes three different programming languages to make the flashy, colorful web pages you see on your screen. All of the text, images, hyperlinks, and functionality of a web page are written in these languages that your browser reads and pulls together to present a complete, stylized page to you. Below is a basic understanding of each of them.

## HTML

HTML stands for HyperText Markup Language, and it deals primarily with the text portion of what you see in your browser. Every web page is actually an HTML file that contains ordinary text (the web page's content) along with HTML tags that tell your browser about the organization and hierarchy of the basic content on your screen.

HTML...

*contains the text showing up on the screen*

*structures the order of content on the page*

*can nest content inside of other content*

*identifies portions of the content by name*

## CSS

CSS stands for Cascading Style Sheets and it is the language your browser reads to create the look and feel of a web page. The style sheets created using CSS determine the color, size, and position of the text as it appears on your screen.

CSS...

*describes the look and feel of the site*

*adds colors and images*

*aligns all content*

*identifies portions of the content by name*

## JavaScript

JavaScript, sometimes abbreviated to JS, is the programming language commonly used to create the interactive effects of a web page. Anything beyond the basic stylized text on a page (HTML and CSS) is written using JavaScript.

JavaScript...

*sets rules for the behavior of interactive components of the site*

*manages dynamic requests for server information*

To use a restaurant metaphor, HTML is the substance your food is made of: carrots, stuffing, tilapia, the raw ingredients. CSS is how the meal is presented or how photogenic your food looks. How fresh are the carrots? Is the stuffing dressed? Is the tilapia blackened or fried? For the purposes of our metaphor and Stylebot, that's all you need to know. JavaScript won't be necessary.

...

In the next section, I'll show you some real HTML and CSS. In order to best understand how all of this is working, I highly recommend following along in a sandbox (what developers call a safe area to mess around). The best tool I've found to allow you to practice writing HTML and CSS is called CodePen (codepen.io). CodePen provides an easy-to-use interface with separate sections for your HTML and CSS.

## TRY HTML

HTML is written using tags, which you can recognize by their angle brackets <>. HTML tags are the hidden keywords of a web page that tell your browser exactly what content to show and where if fits in the content hierarchy. Most tags have a start and a finish, such as this basic HTML tag:

<html></html>

This tag is the first essential tag an HTML file must contain. The start or opening part (<html>) lets the browser know that everything that follows is part of an HTML file, and the closing part (</html>) signals to the browser the end of the HTML file. Anything and everything that falls between these two symbols are the content of one complete HTML file (i.e., web page).

There are three other essential tags that every HTML file must contain. They include the following:

<head></head>

This tag is called the header. The content between this tag does not actually appear on the web page but instead contains relevant details about the document—such as its title, author, style sheets, etc.—that are important to the programmer but that the web user doesn't really need to see.

### <title></title>

This is the title tag, which signals to the browser that the content that appears inside the tag is the web page's title. The browser displays the title at the top of each site's tab.

### <body></body>

The body tag contains the web page's content. All of the elements of a page—the plain text, the images, the links—must go between the start and finish components of the body tag.

To see these tags in action, go to your browser and open up my website, digitaldetangler.com. If you're using Google Chrome or Internet Explorer, use the hot-key Ctrl+U to view the source code for the Digital Detangler home page. If you're using Safari, it's Cmd+Option+U. (Using a different browser? Try right-clicking anywhere on the page and selecting "View page source.")

Once the source code is open, take a close look. See if you can locate all four of the essential tags of an HTML page. If you have trouble, try using the search hot-key you learned in Chapter 5 to find them.

While you're there, you'll notice a whole lot more than those four essential tags. You're also likely to find some tags that have only one part instead of two; these are called self-closing tags. There's other stuff that we won't dive into, but now you have a basic understanding of the essential HTML tags. Below is a list of some other common tags you'll see when you view HTML source code.

&lt;h1&gt;&lt;/h1&gt;                    &lt;button&gt;&lt;/button&gt;

&lt;h6&gt;&lt;/h6&gt;                    &lt;ul&gt;&lt;/ul&gt;

&lt;p&gt;&lt;/p&gt;                      &lt;li&gt;&lt;/li&gt;

&lt;span&gt;&lt;/span&gt;                &lt;ol&gt;&lt;/ol&gt;

&lt;div&gt;&lt;/div&gt;

So what do all these tags do? Let's find out! Go ahead and open up CodePen if you haven't yet, and get ready to play in your sandbox to create your own handmade web page.

Figure 42  As you input HTML and CSS into CodePen, the results appear beneath your code instructions.

**Add these tags to your HTML section of CodePen:**

<h1>Hello</h1>

<h6>Goodbye</h6>

<p>Shopping</p>

<span>Ask me</span>

<div>hippo</div>

<button>Hard</button>

<ul>

   <li>Beach</li>

   <li>Mountains</li>

</ul>

<ol>

   <li>Hit snooze</li>

   <li>Wake up</li>

   <li>Brush Teeth</li>

</ol>

Great work. Now you've had some hands-on experience with HTML tags. But let's face it: All of the items you've put on your page so far have premade looks and are a bit plain. Before we can jazz them up a bit, I need to explain another feature of tags.

HTML tags can hold additional information in the form of

attributes. The most common attributes are id and class. Let's try them out.

**Add the following code to your HTML in CodePen:**

```
<h1 id="greeting">Hello</h1>

<li class="healthy">Brush Teeth</li>
```

If you add the id and class shown above to your existing HTML, you'll now notice...nothing. It looks just the same. Harrumph. Don't worry, things are about to get colorful.

First, you need to know about one tiny rule. If you see an id, that means that is the only id with that value on the entire page. So, if I built a page and added id="greeting" to one of my tags, I can't add that to any other tags. Class is just the opposite; you can add class="healthy" to as many different tags as you like.

In order to have those attributes—id and class—serve any greater purpose, we're going to need to add some CSS.

## TRY CSS

Now you'll get a chance to explore what CSS can do. Stay in the same web page you've been building using CodePen, and follow the directions below.

**Type this code into the CSS section:**

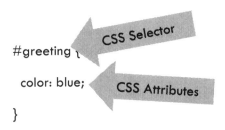

```
#greeting {
    color: blue;
}
```

```
.healthy {

  background-color: green;

}
```

The CSS code above uses a shorthand instruction to add the attributes it contains to dress up the look of your HTML content. The "#" is interpreted as, "Go find an id with whatever comes immediately after the '#.'"

In the same way, the "." is interpreted as, "Go find any items with a class of whatever comes immediately after the '.'"

The CSS selector refers to anything that comes before the curly braces. The CSS selector gives the CSS explicit instructions on which HTML to make beautiful. The part contained by the curly braces can be all sorts of visual instructions, known as CSS attributes. By now you've figured out that the main use of ids and classes is to tell the CSS where to do its thing.

CSS selectors aren't always as simple as the ones shown above. Below, several more advanced ones are shown to give you a sense of how they can be used to target specific HTML tags. Take a moment to try these out in Codepen. Test out ways in which using different CSS selectors will apply the CSS attributes to different sections of your HTML tags.

**HTML**

<h2>Pizza Options</h2>

<ul id="pizzas">

  <li class="meaty">Meat Lovers</li>

  <li class="vegetarian">Veggie Lovers</li>

  <li class="vegetarian">Green Pepper</li>

</ul>

**Working with CSS Selectors**

h2 {

background-color: red;

}

*would select any h2 tags and turn their background-color to red*

Now try swapping out h2 for the CSS selectors below. Notice how changing the CSS selector affects the look of the HTML tags.

ul

*would select any ul tags*

li

*would select any li tags*

#pizzas

*would select the tag with an id of pizzas*

ul#pizzas

*would select the ul tag with an id of pizzas*

.vegetarian

*would select any tags with a class of vegetarian*

li.vegetarian

*would select any li tags with a class of vegetarian*

ul li

*would select any li tags that are inside of a ul tag*

#pizzas li

*would select any li tags that are inside the tag with an id of pizzas*

#pizzas .meaty

*would select any tags with a class of meaty that are inside the tag with an id of pizzas*

As you can see, there are often multiple ways to select the same tags using CSS selectors. How you choose to select tags, sometimes called elements, comes down to personal style and how general or specific you want to be. Remember in math class when your geometry teacher tried to convince you that squares were rectangles but not the other way around? This is the same kind of thing. If you only want to change a particular li tag and not the others, you'll need a specific CSS selector with a class or id. On the other hand, if you want to change the look of every single li tag on the entire site, no need to be specific—li alone would work as your CSS selector.

Play around a bit more in CodePen and see what you can create. There are tons more tutorials online if you are interested in learning more.

Once you are feeling pretty comfortable, head over to Craigslist.com and open up the source code (if you don't remember the hot-keys from when we checked out Digital Detangler's source code earlier, simply right-click anywhere on the page and select "view page source"). This will open up a new page that shows you the HTML and CSS for the Craigslist page in its entirety. As you can expect, it is probably huge, but the best part about Craigslist is that it is pretty readable. You can probably already understand a little bit of what you are looking at. Explore how they've organized the site, where they've used ids, where they've used classes, anything else you find neat. In the next section, we'll put all this new knowledge to use with Stylebot, a revolutionary tool to change the way you view websites from now on.

## STYLEBOT

*Figure 43  The side of the LinkedIn home page with my popularity stats.*

*Figure 44  The same area of the LinkedIn home page after popularity stats have been removed.*

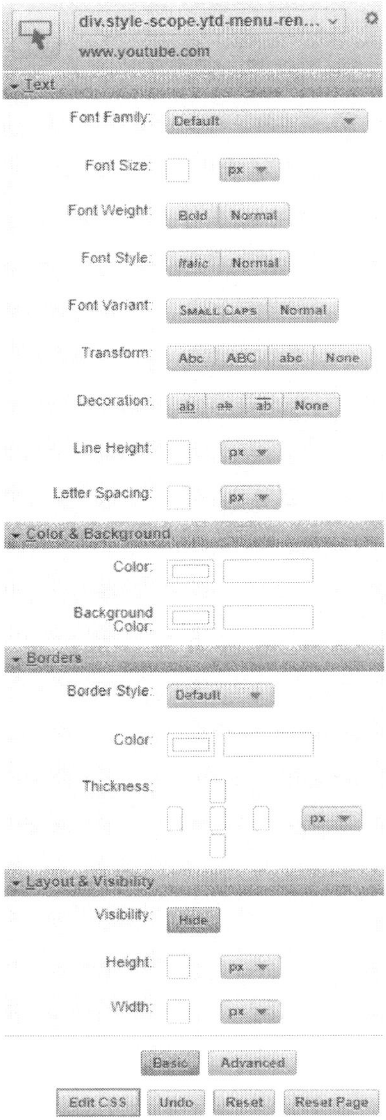

*Figure 45  Stylebot's control panel.*

chrome.google.com/webstore/detail/stylebot/oiaejidbmkiecg bjeifoejpgmdaleoha/

Stylebot is a Chrome extension that gives you the ability to change the appearance of pages you visit regularly. As we'll explore in a moment, Stylebot allows you to add or remove content as you wish to soup up or strip down pages of your choice. I'll begin with the most accessible features before giving you a closer look under the hood.

Once you've installed Stylebot, open up a site you use a lot—I recommend YouTube if you are hoping to follow along with my example below. Open and pause any YouTube video to get started. Verify that Stylebot has been installed; you should see an icon, , containing the letters CSS to the right of the URL. Click on the icon and select "Open Stylebot."

A new control panel should have popped into the right side of your browser. Now, move your mouse around YouTube. As your mouse moves, Stylebot puts a green box around the different sections of the page. Scroll down a bit and once you've gotten the entire comments section bounded by the Stylebot box, click.

Now look back to the Stylebot control panel—something's changed. At the top, where it used to say "Select an Element," it now contains a CSS selector. Further down in the control panel, look for the "Layout and Visibility" section. Inside there is an attribute called "Visibility" with a "Hide" button next to it. Click "Hide," and poof, no more comments on YouTube. Ever. Again.

Imagine the internet without comments. It can be yours. Facebook without other people's reactions. Instagram without knowing how many likes each of your photos gets. Twitter without videos. There are many ways to repeat this process to remove small parts of popular pages and enhance your experience.

Once you've removed a few sections of YouTube—the "Up Next" section is another great target for removal—look to the bottom left corner of the Stylebot control panel. Click on the button labeled "Edit CSS."

Now you are looking at the actual CSS code generated from your clicking on a section and hiding it. In the raw CSS editor, you can make changes as well. Occasionally, the CSS selector that Stylebot automatically chose may be too specific. Look at the CSS selector and try removing sections of the CSS selector. Once you save your changes, you'll be able to see how your changes affected the page.

The more time you spend poking around different sites' HTML and CSS, the more capable you'll become whenever you need to add more specificity with your CSS selectors.

The last mind-blowing feature of Stylebot is that you can embed your own messages into pages. Imagine if Twitter encouraged you to take three calming breaths before you began reading. What if every time you started to sink an hour into Reddit, you saw text cajoling you to write three more pages of your novel? To do this, you have to know about a couple of new CSS attributes that weren't covered previously: font size and content.

Font size allows you to control how large or small the text appears on the screen. The value you assign should be a number followed by px, which stands for pixels. The content attribute's value will be whatever your inspirational text will be, surrounded in quotes.

**The example below works for the Netflix landing page:**

```
div.list-profiles:after {

    color: white;

    font-size: 50px;

    content: "Call a friend instead!";

}
```

Once you open Stylebot and click "Edit CSS," add that code to the page and click "Save." Your Netflix landing page should now look something like this:

*Figure 46 Netflix with my embedded message.*

If you want to do the same thing to other pages, you'll need to find the right CSS selector to insert your message in a nice location on the page. I normally use the Stylebot control panel to select a section of the site close to where I would like my message to appear. Once you select the section, the CSS selector you need is in the drop-down at the top of the control panel. Then click "Edit CSS" and paste the CSS selector and add ":after" to the end of it. Then I'll add color, font size, and content attributes inside curly braces below the CSS selector. If it doesn't work at first, try adjusting the CSS selector, changing the color, or raising the font size.

I hope by now you've grasped the power of restyling pages that you visit frequently. As we covered earlier, images are incredibly powerful and are frequently used to distract us online. Reorganizing our phone setup and installing a few browser tools can go a long way to restoring a sense of calm as you flit from thing to thing. Recall from Chapter 4 that our natural inclination when browsing is to keep jumping around like chipmunks foraging for nuts. Stylebot helps you rebuild an internet where you are less likely to sprint from site to site.

# SET YOUR GOALS

Take a moment to commit to a real change, and get started improving your devices' feng shui.

**If I do not meet my goal, I will give $_____ to _____.**

**My goals:**

   **1.**

   **2.**

Here are a few ideas:

- Build a tools-only homescreen for smartphone.

- Delete any apps that use infinite scroll.

- Try out Space by Dopamine Labs for smartphone.

- Install Textmode to de-image the internet.

- Install Stylebot and use it to clean up two sites.

- Use Stylebot to embed a motivating message on a distracting site.

In the final chapter, you'll finally stop being ruthless with your environment and will start being compassionate towards yourself. Becoming familiar with the benefits of daily gratitude and mindfulness will motivate you to find new ways of thinking about yourself, the world, and your place in it. If you take the time to count your breaths instead of your steps, you may find yourself just a little bit calmer and more resilient when the going gets terrible.

# NINE

## BE: Creating Space for Non-Doing

*Life moves pretty fast. If you don't stop and look around once in a while, you could miss it.*

FERRIS BUELLER'S DAY OFF

The alarm begins playing a relaxing-until-I-started-using-it-as-an-alarm tune a little after 5 a.m. I jerk awake and am in the car, laptop in tow, by 5:25. Having beaten the worst of the traffic, I'm in the water swimming laps at the county rec center by 6. After a quick shower, I hurry to my office. I jog up the stairs, two per stride, because I'm running late. You see, I like to meditate for 20 minutes before I start the day with tea at 7 a.m. in the empty office—most of my coworkers won't arrive for at least two or three more hours. Halfway up the stairs, something stops me. All the things I'm doing are good. Exercise is great. Discipline is great. Working hard is great. But as I stand there in the stairwell, I have a disturbing realization. I am rushing around filling my life so full of healthy lifestyle choices, I am beginning to lose track of myself. Who am I? How do I feel? Those aren't questions I've ever particularly enjoyed answering. I'd rather focus on something "real," something concrete, something measurable. I discover that I've been taking life and slamming

183

him up against the wall, my hands closing around his throat, whispering through clenched teeth, "Where are the *accomplishments?*"

## EAST VS. WEST

Taking a step off the achievatron is a challenging proposition. I am an Eagle Scout, went to a great university, have hiked and biked thousands of miles, visited lots of countries—I don't jump at the chance to stop for a moment to reflect and understand who I am. I'd rather not question why I'm compulsively pushing myself to reach the next level in life. The accomplishments represent what David Brooks has called "resume virtues." He encourages us instead to cultivate "eulogy virtues," the things people will remember about us once we are dead[141]. At its core, I sense that I've spent a long time thinking of myself in these Western terms.

A car is an apt metaphor for a person living with a purely Western mindset. If your car starts to have trouble, you take it in. It may be serious (a blown gasket), or it may be minor (overly worn tires), but the idea is that you get it fixed and get back to whatever you were doing before. To fix the car, we would just need to break it down into concrete steps and start a to-do list to organize the work. After long enough, the car would be in good working condition. That is where the Western mindset excels, when there are problems to solve. There is one drawback, though—this mindset tends to turn our wants into our needs. Consider for a moment that many of the features of your car are not strictly necessary: air conditioning, heat, seat warmers, a back-up camera, Bluetooth-enabled music player, headrest-embedded screens for the kids. This tendency to expand our

---

[141] Brooks, *The Road to Character.*

desires to match our wallets can seduce us into spending large amounts of money on a lot of cool stuff. Unfortunately, we tend to get used to all of the conveniences and continue to have a nagging empty feeling that we are still missing something.

The Eastern mindset has a different metaphor: sandals. Shantideva asks, "Where would there be leather enough to cover the entire world? With just the leather of my sandals, it is as if the whole world were covered. Likewise, I am unable to restrain external phenomena, but I shall restrain my own mind. What need is there to restrain anything else?"[142]

Both perspectives are needed to live a full life. There is important work that needs doing—social injustices to correct, institutional transformations to jumpstart, spouses to love, children to teach—but unless we take moments throughout our lives to course-correct, we'll end up burnt out and bitter.

In the next section, I'll introduce two paths for reflection and, if needed, course-correction. Gratitude and mindfulness practices won't fix all of your problems, but they can make life less of a slog.

## GRATITUDE

There is an old story about a philosopher named Diogenes, who lived in a barrel. He was said to be extraordinarily wise and was sought by many for advice. Alexander the Great, the most powerful man in the world, decided to pay Diogenes a visit and thank him for his contributions to philosophy and science, which weren't different things back then. When Alexander

---

[142] Babauta, "A Practice For When You Find Yourself Annoyed by Other People."

found Diogenes sunning himself next to his mangy barrel, Diogenes doesn't appear to be overly affected by being in the presence of such a powerful figure. Alexander tells Diogenes, "Name your desire, anything you wish, and I will make it so." Diogenes pauses, thinks, and then answers, "Please step a bit to the left; you are blocking the sun."

There are a number of possible conclusions to draw from that story, but I'd like to focus on the way Diogenes was tuned to the present. He was appreciating the sun's light so much that Alexander's greatness paled in comparison. Alexander had enormous human power, yet he could never give Diogenes the wonderful feeling of sun warming his body after a chilly night. For Diogenes, the truly sublime couldn't be bought or commodified. The sun was a gift that was not always available, so when it warmed him gently, that was a moment worth savoring. Often in our lives, we miss opportunities to savor moments. Weeks after buying a new car, or moving into a larger apartment, or switching to a pricey shampoo, we get used to the change and no longer derive joy from the improvement. This process of getting used to your life and needing constant improvements to stay happy has been called the hedonic treadmill[143]. It reminds me of when my dad taught me to swim. He would move farther and farther from me as I swam toward him. Happiness, in the same way, can seem perpetually out of reach.

The only sustainable way to keep ourselves in a state of gratitude is to build a daily practice that forces us to appreciate the good things in life. In no way should this practice act as a denial of the heartache and pain that we all suffer; instead, it is simply a call

---

[143] Calvo and Peters, *Positive Computing.*

to allow both to coexist. You can have cancer and enjoy mint chocolate chip ice cream. You can lose a loved one and laugh at a friend's joke.

To give you an example of how you can begin a gratitude practice, take a moment to write a thank-you note, as described in the next section.

**Choose an item, and write a thank-you note to the item in the space below.**

well-made furniture                    clothes

car                                                    trash service

kitchen appliance                      grocery store

group of people                          your own idea

Writing a thank-you note is one way of expressing appreciation, but there are many more. Feel free to come up with your own ideas. The key is to create a daily habit of completing some practice or activity to bring about awareness of the good things around you. A few of my suggestions include:

- List things you're thankful for (the Thanksgiving option).

- Write a gratitude letter to a loved one (a yearbook-style entry for adults).

- Give someone a small treat (flowers or chocolate work well).

- Tell a manager about something that went well (customer service managers are used to interacting with people in terrible moods—be the exception).

At this point, I hope you value being grateful for its own sake. If you still aren't convinced, though, consider that daily gratitude practices have been clinically demonstrated to increase compassion, joy, generosity, optimism, and happiness. Other benefits include more exercising and improved immune support, along with less loneliness and fewer trips to the doctor[144].

## MINDFULNESS

Meditation has been developed over thousands of years. Originally meditation fell within the domain of religion—primarily Buddhists but also mystics of many stripes. In recent decades, meditation practices have been secularized to allow more people to experience their transformative power. Jon Kabat-Zinn remains an icon of this new secularized form of

---

[144] "In Praise of Gratitude"; Emmons, "Why Gratitude Is Good."

meditation, often referred to as mindfulness. Kabat-Zinn defines mindfulness as "paying attention in a particular way, on purpose, in the present moment, and nonjudgmentally"[145]. The two tools below are great jumping-off points if you are ready to start a mindfulness practice.

## Stop, Breathe & Think

stopbreathethink.com

This app is great for beginners and has short guided meditations to get you started. Over time, you can expand your practice to include longer meditations with or without guidance.

## Insight Timer

insighttimer.com

Insight Timer is the most popular meditation app in the world. It allows teachers of every kind to upload guided meditations and provides a tool for configuring your own meditations. Whether you are looking for a Christian contemplative prayer meditation or are hoping to find some music to align your chakras, it is all here.

## Practice Meditation

Below, you'll find a mindfulness meditation that was created with digital interruptions in mind. It's intended to be done in a group where one person reads the script aloud. The idea is that by introducing digital sounds during meditation—sounds that normally jolt us into fight-or-flight mode—over time you will cultivate a more relaxed response to life's dings, beeps, pings,

---

[145] Delagran and Haley, "What Is Mindfulness?"

and buzzes.

## Meditation Script

Take a deep breath.

Find a comfortable seated position on a chair or pillow.

Make sure your back is straight, but your shoulders are relaxed.

You may place your hands on your knees or on your lap.

Today's meditation is going to focus on the breath. You will be breathing naturally, allowing yourself to observe the rhythm and quality of your breath as it flows into and out of your body.

As we meditate, you will begin to hear some interruptive sounds. If you notice those sounds interrupting you, that is okay. Rather than be frustrated or angry with yourself, simply notice that you were distracted and take your attention back to the breath. Becoming distracted is completely normal. The practice today is to continue bringing yourself back to the breath after your mind wanders. Take a few breaths, and settle into a state of relaxation.

[Pause for a few minutes.]

For the first series of breaths, we are going to take air in through our noses and out through our mouths. Breathe in through your nose, breathe out through your mouth. Breathe in through your nose, breathe out through your mouth. Breathe in through your nose, breathe out through your mouth. Continue on your own.

[Pause for a few minutes. Introduce digital interruptions at random intervals.]

For the next series of breaths, we are going to breathe into and out of our noses. Breathe in through your nose, breathe out through your nose—count one. Breathe in through your nose, breathe out through your nose—count two. Continue on your own.

[Pause for a few minutes. Introduce digital interruptions at random intervals.]

To finish, we are going to take three deep breaths in whatever way feels most natural for you. Breathe in, breathe out. Breathe in, breathe out. Breathe in, breathe out.

Take a moment to transition back into an awareness of your surroundings. Wiggle your fingers and toes. When you are ready, slowly open your eyes.

Thank you. Calmness is strength.

[Ring bell.]

...

Once you've started a daily mindfulness practice, you'll likely start to notice qualitative benefits, but you'll also experience measurable improvements like those demonstrated by the University of Massachusetts Medical School. Among other benefits, mindfulness practices significantly improve anxiety, panic attacks, work-family-financial stress, depression, sleep problems, and cancer[146].

---

146 "FAQs - MBSR - MBCT."

I want to make sure I'm clear, though; in the studies involving medical patients, participants continued taking conventional medicine. If you have cancer, don't stop taking meds in exchange for meditation; take your meds and also meditate.

An often-recommended mindfulness dosage is 40 minutes per day, which can seem daunting. If so, start smaller and build up. You can also split up the time into two or more meditations throughout the day. I recommend meditating sometime in the morning and then meditating just before dinner to help transition out of your busy day and into your home.

## CONCLUSION

Since that moment in the stairwell of a soulless office building, I left the software world to focus on helping others find healthy ways to use technology—ways that don't leave them feeling empty and burnt out. I've had many conversations about mindful ways to use technology with a variety of folks. Whether on the telephone, Skype, or Zoom, in offices, bars, universities, or a secondary school, we are eager to talk about technology. Every time I speak with others about their relationships with technology, they begin by making personal statements about their own struggles.

We all know that technology is new and sexy and awesome, but it also changes us. And if you don't like the way it changes you or don't feel in control, don't hunker down with those evil twins: shame and guilt. Change the way you use technology. Don't beat yourself up; doing so doesn't work anyway[147]. But don't ignore it. Use the tools covered in this book to arm yourself against

---

[147] Cooper, "Why Rest Is so Important (and Why You're Not Getting Enough)."

distractions that attempt to draw you away from your intentions.

The way you spend your time ultimately defines who you are and who you become. What could be more important?

# ACKNOWLEDGEMENTS

Many people, some knowingly, have helped create the book before you. Thanks to Katherine Watkins for being the first graduate of the Digital Detangler course and for providing tremendously useful feedback. Melanie Gao provided strategic insight early on and dared me to write the book. Jack Dunlap asked me lots of questions that matter, while Sally Levy was a constant encourager and an engaged test subject. Linda Dunlap, aka Mom, forced us to read as children but also let us ride our bicycles unsupervised. My dad has never stopped demanding that I excel in whatever I do, even while cancer was attempting to kill him. Andrew Britt has been a steadfast encourager since we started meeting weekly a year ago. Alex Myers and I became adults together, and he continues to push me to think carefully about the message I spread. David and Emily Frazelle provided thoughtful complaints about email years ago when I lived with them and their 18-month-old. Jed Macosko and Alan Huffman deserve credit for inspiring Chapter 5. Gerry Andrade and Chris Gerding have given practical business advice. Dylan Jackson saved the day with some last-minute creative heroics. Nathan Baldwin was the Apple specialist and a source of much-needed distracting adventures. Christina Crook, author of *The Joy of Missing Out*, has been supportive of the course, and it has been great to see the way she focuses on what you get when you disconnect. Brother-sister duo Zack and Kelly Bradford provided a much-needed college perspective on materials. Andrew Dunn of Siempo and Chris Dancy were willing to have conversations with me that shaped and led to my diving into the mindful technology movement headfirst. Brian Arenz and Peter Himmelreich drank beers with me and went deep into my head, separating what is real from what I think. Dr. Larry Rosen and Holland Haiis provided thoughtful commentary on smartphones and human-computer interaction. The entire team at RescueTime, which had the audacity to build a cloud-based app with a delete button that actually deletes, deserves props. Robby Macdonell, who runs RescueTime, listens well and knows more about focus and technology than anyone else I know. Robert Plotkin and Liza Kindred both lead incredible movements toward conscious, intentional technology use. Katherine Drotos Cuthbert and Malika Isler are luminaries at their universities, where they encourage students to question the status quo and to make their mental health a priority. Nicholas Carr, Sherry Turkle, and Tristan Harris inspire from afar. Cal Newport, Manoush Zomorodi, and Adam Atler pushed this issue to new places. Jack Reeves got me to get serious about controlling my internet connection. Jennifer Chesak provided much-needed coaching throughout the publishing process. Carmen Toussaint and Rivendell Writers' Colony shut out the rest of the world and got me to finish the book. John Moore lit up what would have been a dour two weeks of intensive writing. April Williams and Cameron Dunlap edited this book into something readable. Cameron provided untold amounts of encouragement and comfort during what have seemed like insurmountable challenges. While writing, I've listened to local birds and airplanes, as well as Taylor Swift, The Wild Reeds, Alt-J, Mandolin Orange, and Local Natives. Undoubtedly, I've left some folks out; they are appreciated just the same.

# REFERENCES

Acar, Güneş, Brendan Van Alsenoy, Frank Piessens, Claudia
    Diaz, and Bart Preneel. "Facebook Tracking Through
    Social Plug-Ins," June 24, 2015, 24.

"Alphabet Announces Second Quarter 2017 Results."
    Alphabet Investor Relations, July 24, 2017.
    https://abc.xyz/investor/news/earnings/2017/Q2_al
    phabet_earnings/.

Alter, Adam. *Irresistible: The Rise of Addictive Technology and the
    Business of Keeping Us Hooked.* Reprint edition. Penguin
    Books, 2018.

"American Time Use Survey: Charts by Topic: Leisure and
    Sports Activities." Bureau of Labor Statistics,
    December 20, 2016.
    https://www.bls.gov/TUS/CHARTS/LEISURE.HT
    M.

"Are You a Nomophobe?" Iowa State University - News
    Service, August 26, 2015.
    https://www.news.iastate.edu/news/2015/08/26/no
    mophobia.

"Average U.S. Employee Only Takes Half of Earned Vacation
    Time; Glassdoor Employment Confidence Survey (Q1
    2014)." Glassdoor Blog, April 3, 2014.
    https://www.glassdoor.com/blog/average-employee-
    takes-earned-vacation-time-glassdoor-employment-
    confidence-survey-q1-2014/.

Babauta, Leo. "A Practice For When You Find Yourself
    Annoyed by Other People." zen habits, February 19,
    2018. https://zenhabits.net/annoyed/.

Bartlett, Jamie. *The Dark Net: Inside the Digital Underworld.*
    Brooklyn: Melville House, 2015.

Blanding, Michael. "The Business of Behavioral Economics."
    Harvard Business School Business Research for
    Business Leaders, August 11, 2014.

http://hbswk.hbs.edu/item/the-business-of-behavioral-economics.

"Blue Light Has a Dark Side." Harvard Health, December 30, 2017. https://www.health.harvard.edu/staying-healthy/blue-light-has-a-dark-side.

Brooks, Chad, Business News Daily Senior Writer May 17, and 2017 07:17 am EST. "Checking Email After Work Won't Make You Miserable." Business News Daily, May 17, 2017. https://www.businessnewsdaily.com/7754-email-after-hours.html.

Brooks, David. *The Road to Character*. Reprint edition. Random House Trade Paperbacks, 2016.

"Browser Market Share." Market Share Statistics for Internet Technologies. Accessed May 18, 2018. https://www.netmarketshare.com/browser-market-share.aspx.

Burkeman, Oliver. "This Column Will Change Your Life: Get into the Habit of Random Rewards." *The Guardian*, April 22, 2011, sec. Life and style. http://www.theguardian.com/lifeandstyle/2011/apr/23/this-column-change-life-random-rewards.

Calvo, Rafael A., and Dorian Peters. *Positive Computing: Technology for Wellbeing and Human Potential*. Cambridge, Massachusetts: The MIT Press, 2014.

Carnegie, Dale. *How To Enjoy Your Life And Your Job*. New York: Pocket Books, 1990.

Carr, Nicholas. "How Smartphones Hijack Our Minds." The Wall Street Journal, October 6, 2017. https://www.wsj.com/articles/how-smartphones-hijack-our-minds-1507307811.

———. *The Shallows: What the Internet Is Doing to Our Brains*. First Edition. New York, NY: W. W. Norton & Company, 2010.

———. *Utopia Is Creepy: And Other Provocations*. First Edition. W. W. Norton & Company, 2017.

Cirillo, Francesco. "The Pomodoro Technique®." Accessed

May 18, 2018.
https://francescocirillo.com/pages/pomodoro-technique.

"Comcast Time Warner Cable Merger Video." C-SPAN.org, May 8, 2014. https://www.c-span.org/video/?319101-1/comcast-time-warner-cable-merger&start=4527.

Conger, Kate. "Uber Begins Background Collection of Rider Location Data." *TechCrunch* (blog), November 29, 2016.
http://social.techcrunch.com/2016/11/28/uber-background-location-data-collection/.

Cooper, Belle. "Why Rest Is so Important (and Why You're Not Getting Enough)." *RescueTime Blog* (blog), September 12, 2017.
https://blog.rescuetime.com/rest/.

Davies, Madlen. "We Now Spend More Time on Phones and Laptops than We Do SLEEPING." Mail Online, March 11, 2015.
http://www.dailymail.co.uk/health/article-2989952/How-technology-taking-lives-spend-time-phones-laptops-SLEEPING.html.

Delagran, Louise, and Alex Haley. "What Is Mindfulness?" Taking Charge of Your Health & Wellbeing. Accessed May 18, 2018.
https://www.takingcharge.csh.umn.edu/what-mindfulness.

Diamond, Dan. "Just 8% of People Achieve Their New Year's Resolutions. Here's How They Do It." Forbes, January 1, 2013.
https://www.forbes.com/sites/dandiamond/2013/01/01/just-8-of-people-achieve-their-new-years-resolutions-heres-how-they-did-it/.

Duhigg, Charles. *The Power of Habit: Why We Do What We Do in Life and Business.* New York: Random House Trade Paperbacks, 2014.

Eler, Alicia. "Study: Average App Session Lasts About 1 Minute." *ReadWrite* (blog), January 17, 2012.

https://readwrite.com/2012/01/17/study_average_a
pp_session_lasts_about_1_minute/.

Emmons, Robert. "Why Gratitude Is Good." Greater Good
Magazine, November 16, 2010.
https://greatergood.berkeley.edu/article/item/why_gr
atitude_is_good.

"Facebook Reports Second Quarter 2017 Results." Facebook,
July 26, 2017. https://investor.fb.com/investor-
news/press-release-details/2017/Facebook-Reports-
Second-Quarter-2017-Results/default.aspx.

"FAQs - MBSR - MBCT." University of Massachusetts
Medical School, February 17, 2014.
https://umassmed.edu/cfm/mindfulness-based-
programs/faqs-mbsr-mbct/.

Flood, Alison. "Book up for a Longer Life: Readers Die Later,
Study Finds." *The Guardian*, August 8, 2016, sec.
Books.
http://www.theguardian.com/books/2016/aug/08/b
ook-up-for-a-longer-life-readers-die-later-study-finds.

Galloway, Scott. *The Four: The Hidden DNA of Amazon, Apple,
Facebook, and Google*. First Edition. New York:
Portfolio, 2017.

Ganster, Daniel, Leslie Hammer, Jessica Streit, Michelle Lee,
Naomi Swanson, Heidi Hudson, and Jeannie Nigam.
"Intervening for Work Stress: Work-Life Stress and
Total Worker Health Approaches." *CDC NIOSH
Science Blog* (blog), November 7, 2014.
https://blogs.cdc.gov/niosh-science-
blog/2014/11/17/stress-webinar/.

Gardner, Amanda. "TV Watching Raises Risk of Health
Problems, Dying Young." CNN, June 14, 2011.
http://www.cnn.com/2011/HEALTH/06/14/tv.wat
ching.unhealthy/index.html.

Gaudette, Emily. "Netflix Declares War on Sleep, Its Biggest
'Competitor.'" Newsweek, November 6, 2017.
http://www.newsweek.com/netflix-binge-watch-
sleep-deprivation-703029.

Gazzaley, Adam, and Larry D. Rosen. *The Distracted Mind: Ancient Brains in a High-Tech World.* Reprint edition. S.l.: The MIT Press, 2017.

Goel, Vindu. "Facebook Tinkers With Users' Emotions in News Feed Experiment, Stirring Outcry." *The New York Times*, December 20, 2017, sec. Technology. https://www.nytimes.com/2014/06/30/technology/facebook-tinkers-with-users-emotions-in-news-feed-experiment-stirring-outcry.html.

Goitein, Elizabeth, and David M. Shapiro. "Reducing Overclassification Through Accountability." Brennan Center for Justice, October 5, 2011. https://www.brennancenter.org/publication/reducing-overclassification-through-accountability.

Golbeck, Jennifer. *Your Social Media "Likes" Expose More than You Think.* Accessed June 1, 2018. https://www.ted.com/talks/jennifer_golbeck_the_curly_fry_conundrum_why_social_media_likes_say_more_than_you_might_think.

Goldhill, Olivia. "Multitasking Is Scientifically Impossible, so Give up Now." *The Telegraph*, April 2, 2015, sec. Women. https://www.telegraph.co.uk/women/womens-life/11512469/Multitasking-is-scientifically-impossible-so-give-up-nowMultitask.html.

Harris, Tristan. "Distracted in 2016? Reboot Your Phone with Mindfulness," January 27, 2016. http://www.tristanharris.com/2016/01/distracted-in-2016-welcome-to-mindfulness-bootcamp-for-your-iphone/.

Hills, Suzannah. "Whatever Happened to the Lunch Hour? How Breaks Have Been Reduced to Just 29 Minutes Because We're Too Busy." Daily Mail, January 25, 2013. http://www.dailymail.co.uk/news/article-2268092/Whatever-happened-lunch-hour-How-breaks-reduced-just-29-minutes-busy.html.

"How Much Time Do People Spend on Their Mobile Phones

in 2017?" Hacker Noon, May 9, 2017.
https://hackernoon.com/how-much-time-do-people-spend-on-their-mobile-phones-in-2017-e5f90a0b10a6.

"How to Live Without Google." DuckDuckGo Blog, September 14, 2017. https://spreadprivacy.com/how-to-remove-google/.

Ilardi, Stephen. "Why Personal Tech Is Depressing." *Wall Street Journal*, October 26, 2017, sec. Life. https://www.wsj.com/articles/why-personal-tech-is-depressing-1509026300.

"In Praise of Gratitude." Harvard Health, November 2011. https://www.health.harvard.edu/newsletter_article/in-praise-of-gratitude.

Ingraham, Christopher. "Chart: The Animals That Are Most Likely to Kill You This Summer." *Washington Post*, June 16, 2015, sec. Wonkblog. https://www.washingtonpost.com/news/wonk/wp/2015/06/16/chart-the-animals-that-are-most-likely-to-kill-you-this-summer/.

Isaac, Mike. "Facebook Offers Tools for Those Who Fear a Friend May Be Suicidal." *The New York Times*, December 21, 2017, sec. Technology. https://www.nytimes.com/2016/06/15/technology/facebook-offers-tools-for-those-who-fear-a-friend-may-be-suicidal.html.

Jones, Julia, and Eve Bower. "American Deaths in Terrorism vs. Gun Violence in One Graph." CNN, December 30, 2015. https://www.cnn.com/2015/10/02/us/oregon-shooting-terrorism-gun-violence/index.html.

"Kaspersky Lab Study Proves Smartphones Distract Workers and Decrease Productivity." Kaspersky Lab US, August 26, 2016. https://usa.kaspersky.com/about/press-releases/2016_kaspersky-lab-study-proves-smartphones-distract-workers-and-decrease-productivity.

Keller, William W. *Democracy Betrayed: The Rise of the Surveillance Security State.* Berkeley, CA: Counterpoint, 2017.

Lanier, Jaron. "Opinion | Should Facebook Manipulate Users?" *The New York Times*, December 20, 2017, sec. Opinion. https://www.nytimes.com/2014/07/01/opinion/jaron-lanier-on-lack-of-transparency-in-facebook-study.html.

Lapowsky, Issie. "How Facebook Knows You Better Than Your Friends Do." WIRED, January 13, 2015. https://www.wired.com/2015/01/facebook-personality-test/.

Latson, Jennifer. "A Cure for Disconnection." Psychology Today, March 7, 2018. https://www.psychologytoday.com/articles/201803/cure-disconnection.

Lin, Helen Lee. "How Your Cell Phone Hurts Your Relationships." Scientific American, September 4, 2012. https://www.scientificamerican.com/article/how-your-cell-phone-hurts-your-relationships/.

Luckerson, Victor. "Is Lunch a Waste of Time — or a Productivity Booster?" *Time*, July 16, 2012. http://business.time.com/2012/07/16/the-lunch-hour-necessity-or-nuisance/.

Lynch, Michael P. *The Internet of Us: Knowing More and Understanding Less in the Age of Big Data.* First Edition. New York: Liveright, 2016.

Maheshwari, Sapna. "That Game on Your Phone May Be Tracking What You're Watching on TV." *The New York Times*, January 4, 2018, sec. Business Day. https://www.nytimes.com/2017/12/28/business/media/alphonso-app-tracking.html.

McDermott, Nicole. "Is Long-Term Stress Affecting Your Fertility?," March 25, 2014. https://www.refinery29.com/2014/03/65083/women-fertility-stress.

McNamee, David. "How Does Facebook Affect Our Sense of Belonging?" Medical News Today, May 12, 2014. https://www.medicalnewstoday.com/articles/276656.php.

Meeker, Mary. "2017 Internet Trends Report," May 31, 2017. http://www.kpcb.com/internet-trends.

"Mobile Metrix." comScore, Inc. Accessed May 18, 2018. http://www.comscore.com/Products/Audience-Analytics/Mobile-Metrix.

Munroe, Randall. "Xkcd: Settled." Accessed May 18, 2018. https://xkcd.com/1235/.

Nakashima, Ryan, and Mae Anderson. "How Facebook Was Able to Siphon off Phone Call and Text Logs." USA TODAY, March 27, 2018. https://www.usatoday.com/story/tech/news/2018/03/27/how-facebook-able-siphon-off-phone-call-and-text-logs/464656002/.

Neal, Meghan. "Stress Levels Soar in America by up to 30% in 30 Years." NY Daily News, June 16, 2012. http://www.nydailynews.com/news/national/stress-levels-soar-america-30-30-years-article-1.1096918.

Newport, Cal. Deep Work: Rules for Focused Success in a Distracted World. First Edition. New York: Grand Central Publishing, 2016.

"NSA Leaker Edward Snowden In His Own Words: 'You're Being Watched.'" Democracy Now!, July 4, 2013. http://www.democracynow.org/2013/7/4/nsa_leaker_edward_snowden_in_his.

"Obama Criticizes His Rivals on Iraq." Boston.Com, March 20, 2008. http://archive.boston.com/news/nation/articles/2008/03/20/obama_criticizes_his_rivals_on_iraq/.

O'Neil, Cathy. Weapons of Math Destruction: How Big Data Increases Inequality and Threatens Democracy. First Edition. New York: Crown, 2016.

"Overweight & Obesity Statistics | NIDDK." National Institute of Diabetes and Digestive and Kidney

Diseases. Accessed May 18, 2018.
https://www.niddk.nih.gov/health-
information/health-statistics/overweight-obesity.

Pariser, Eli. *The Filter Bubble: How the New Personalized Web Is Changing What We Read and How We Think.* Reprint edition. New York, NY: Penguin Books, 2012.

Perry, Keith. "Stress Can Be Transmitted through TV Screen," May 1, 2014, sec. News.
https://www.telegraph.co.uk/news/science/10802814/Stress-can-be-transmitted-through-TV-screen.html.

Price, Catherine. *How to Break Up with Your Phone: The 30-Day Plan to Take Back Your Life.* California: Ten Speed Press, 2018.

"Privacy Mythbusting #6: Security Equals Privacy. (Nope!)." DuckDuckGo Blog, July 25, 2017.
https://spreadprivacy.com/security-is-not-privacy/.

Pullen, Liz. "Yes, Men Can Be Victims of Online Harassment. But in Reality, Women Have It Much Worse." *Washington Post*, October 28, 2014, sec. PostEverything.
https://www.washingtonpost.com/posteverything/wp/2014/10/28/yes-men-can-be-victims-of-online-harassment-but-in-reality-women-have-it-much-worse/.

Purcell, Kristen, Joanna Brenner, and Lee Rainie. "Search Engine Use 2012." *Pew Research Center: Internet, Science & Tech* (blog), March 9, 2012.
http://www.pewinternet.org/2012/03/09/search-engine-use-2012/.

"Q2 2017 Letter to Shareholders." Twitter, July 27, 2017.
http://files.shareholder.com/downloads/AMDA-2F526X/6164560397x0x951006/4D8EE364-9CC3-4386-A872-ACCD9C5034CF/Q217_Shareholder_Letter.pdf.

Roberts, Jeff John. "Yahoo Got Hacked Big Time: What You Need to Know." Fortune, September 22, 2016.
http://fortune.com/2016/09/22/yahoo-hack-qa/.

Robinson, Jennifer, and Alex Pentland. "Workplace Socializing Is Productive." Gallup.com, November 13, 2008. http://news.gallup.com/businessjournal/111766/News-Flash-Workplace-Socializing-Productive.aspx.

Rock, David. *Your Brain at Work: Strategies for Overcoming Distraction, Regaining Focus, and Working Smarter All Day Long.* First Edition. New York: HarperBusiness, 2009.

Rodriguez, Tori. "Negative Emotions Are Key to Well-Being." Scientific American, May 1, 2013. https://doi.org/10.1038/scientificamericanmind0513-26.

Rosen, Dennis. "Watching TV Leads to Obesity." Psychology Today, August 13, 2009. http://www.psychologytoday.com/blog/sleeping-angels/200908/watching-tv-leads-obesity.

Rubin, Gretchen. "Get More Bang for Your Happiness Buck: Revel in Anticipation." Psychology Today, February 12, 2011. http://www.psychologytoday.com/blog/the-happiness-project/201102/get-more-bang-your-happiness-buck-revel-in-anticipation.

Scheer, Robert. *They Know Everything About You: How Data-Collecting Corporations and Snooping Government Agencies Are Destroying Democracy.* New York: Nation Books, 2015.

Schor, Juliet. *The Overworked American: The Unexpected Decline Of Leisure.* First Edition. New York, NY: Basic Books, 1992.

Schulson, Michael. "If the Internet Is Addictive, Why Don't We Regulate It?" Aeon, November 24, 2015. https://aeon.co/essays/if-the-internet-is-addictive-why-don-t-we-regulate-it.

Schumacher, E. F. *A Guide for the Perplexed.* Reissue edition. Harper Perennial, 2015.

Specktor, Brandon. "Here's Why Your Brain Needs You to Read Every Day." *Reader's Digest* (blog), December 22, 2017. https://www.rd.com/culture/benefits-of-reading/.

Stephen, Bijan. "You Won't Believe How Little Americans Read." Time, June 22, 2014. http://time.com/2909743/americans-reading/.

Sullivan, Gail. "Sheryl Sandberg Not Sorry for Facebook Mood Manipulation Study." *Washington Post*, July 3, 2014, sec. Morning Mix. https://www.washingtonpost.com/news/morning-mix/wp/2014/07/03/sheryl-sandberg-not-sorry-for-facebook-mood-manipulation-study/.

Sullivan, Sean. "NSA Head: Surveillance Helped Thwart More than 50 Terror Plots." *Washington Post*, June 18, 2013, sec. Post Politics. https://www.washingtonpost.com/news/post-politics/wp/2013/06/18/nsa-head-surveillance-helped-thwart-more-than-50-terror-attempts/?utm_term=.bd299c1ea56a.

Taplin, Jonathan. *Move Fast and Break Things: How Facebook, Google, and Amazon Cornered Culture and Undermined Democracy*. New York: Little, Brown and Company, 2017.

"Television Watching and 'Sit Time.'" Harvard T. H. Chan School of Public Health Obesity Prevention Source, October 21, 2012. https://www.hsph.harvard.edu/obesity-prevention-source/obesity-causes/television-and-sedentary-behavior-and-obesity/.

"The Research." Project: Time Off. Accessed May 18, 2018. https://projecttimeoff.com/sites/default/files/PTO_SoAV%20Report_FINAL.pdf.

"The U.S. Digital Consumer Report." Accessed March 30, 2018. http://www.nielsen.com/us/en/insights/reports/2014/the-us-digital-consumer-report.

Thompson, Clive. *Smarter Than You Think: How Technology Is Changing Our Minds for the Better*. New York: Penguin Press, 2013.

Timberg, Craig. "U.S. Threatened Massive Fine to Force Yahoo to Release Data." *Washington Post*, September 11, 2014, sec. Technology. https://www.washingtonpost.com/business/technolo gy/us-threatened-massive-fine-to-force-yahoo-to-release-data/2014/09/11/38a7f69e-39e8-11e4-9c9f-ebb47272e40e_story.html.

Tromholt, Morten. "The Facebook Experiment: Quitting Facebook Leads to Higher Levels of Well-Being." *Cyberpsychology, Behavior, and Social Networking* 19 (November 1, 2016): 661–66. https://doi.org/10.1089/cyber.2016.0259.

Turkle, Sherry. *Alone Together: Why We Expect More from Technology and Less from Each Other.* Expanded, Revised edition. New York etc.: Basic Books, 2017.

Twenge, Jean. *IGen: Why Today's Super-Connected Kids Are Growing Up Less Rebellious, More Tolerant, Less Happy-and Completely Unprepared for Adulthood-and What That Means for the Rest of Us.* 2nd Print edition. New York: Atria Books, 2017.

"US Digital Ad Spending to Surpass TV This Year - EMarketer," September 13, 2016. https://www.emarketer.com/Article/US-Digital-Ad-Spending-Surpass-TV-this-Year/1014469.

Volpi, David. "Heavy Technology Use Linked to Fatigue, Stress and Depression in Young Adults." *Huffington Post* (blog), August 2, 2012. https://www.huffingtonpost.com/david-volpi-md-pc-facs/technology-depression_b_1723625.html.

Wahba, Phil. "Amazon Is the King of Online Retail and It's Not Even Close." Fortune, November 6, 2015. http://fortune.com/2015/11/06/amazon-retailers-ecommerce/.

Ward, Adrian F., Kristen Duke, Ayelet Gneezy, and Maarten W. Bos. "Brain Drain: The Mere Presence of One's Own Smartphone Reduces Available Cognitive Capacity." *Journal of the Association for Consumer Research*

2, no. 2 (April 1, 2017): 140–54.
https://doi.org/10.1086/691462.

Weissmann, Jordan. "Americans, Ever Hateful of Leisure, Are More Likely to Work Nights and Weekends." *Slate*, September 11, 2014.
https://www.slate.com/blogs/moneybox/2014/09/1 1/u_s_work_life_balance_americans_are_more_likely _to_work_nights_and_weekends.html.

Woollaston, Victoria. "How Often Do YOU Look at Your Phone? The Average User Now Picks up Their Device More than 1,500 Times a Week." Mail Online, October 8, 2014.
http://www.dailymail.co.uk/sciencetech/article-2783677/How-YOU-look-phone-The-average-user-picks-device-1-500-times-day.html.

"WORKING HARD OR HARDLY WORKING? Employees Waste More Than One Day a Week on Non-Work Activities," July 19, 2017.
https://www.prnewswire.com/news-releases/working-hard-or-hardly-working-employees-waste-more-than-one-day-a-week-on-non-work-activities-300490524.html.

# ABOUT THE AUTHOR

Pete Dunlap grew up in North Carolina, where he earned degrees in physics and education. He taught internationally for four years, before spending another four building software. Today, Pete lives with his wife and two rabbits in Nashville, where he founded Digital Detangler and created ScrollStopper. Pete speaks and teaches about digital wellness at universities and corporations. Part storyteller, part nerd, part MacGyver, Pete relates to each audience and packs his presentations full of practical takeaways. For more information, visit digitaldetangler.com.

Made in the USA
Lexington, KY
12 January 2019